In a world that so easily scatters our attention, *The Perfection of God's Words* is a simple, powerful call to refocus. It's a reminder for us to pause and reflect on the beautiful power of God's words displayed in Scripture and spilling forward into our own lives. As my grandfather, John Troyer has been this reminder for me more times than I can count. This book is simply an extension of his heart.

—Victor Hesser
Pastor Resident, North Park Community Church
Eugene, Oregon

John has a unique way of helping Scripture come alive. His thoughtful reflections invite you to slow down, listen, and let God's word shape your heart. This devotional reflects both his depth of insight and his genuine love for Jesus.

—Rev. Dan MacGillivray
Lead Pastor, Fort St. John Alliance Church
Fort St. John, B.C.

This devotional is an excellent resource that explains the creation, purpose, and meaning of life. It shows everyone how much God loves them and that devotion to Him brings protection and life. It's a good resource for unbelievers because it talks about the mission of Jesus, who came from heaven to meet His disciples and teach them through the resurrection and saving people from their sins. Above all, it speaks of the powerful word of God and its transforming power.

—Johny A Giesbrecht
Missionary Pastor

— 100 DAILY DEVOTIONALS —

THE PERFECTION OF God's WORDS

JOHN TROYER

THE PERFECTION OF GOD'S WORDS: 100 DAILY DEVOTIONALS
Copyright © 2025 by John Troyer

All rights reserved. Neither this publication nor any part of this publication may be reproduced or transmitted in any form or by any means, electronic or mechanical, including photocopying, recording or any information storage and retrieval system, without permission in writing from the author.

Unless otherwise indicated, scripture quotations taken from the Holy Bible, King James Version, which is in the public domain. Scripture quotations marked MSG are taken from The Message, copyright © 1993, 2002, 2018 by Eugene H. Peterson. Used by permission of NavPress. All rights reserved. Represented by Tyndale House Publishers. Scripture quotations marked (NLT) are taken from the Holy Bible, New Living Translation, copyright ©1996, 2004, 2015 by Tyndale House Foundation. Used by permission of Tyndale House Publishers, Carol Stream, Illinois 60188. All rights reserved. Scripture taken from the New King James Version®. Copyright © 1982 by Thomas Nelson. Used by permission. All rights reserved. Scripture taken from the New Century Version®. Copyright © 2005 by Thomas Nelson. Used by permission. All rights reserved. Scripture quotations taken from the (NASB®) New American Standard Bible®, Copyright © 1960, 1971, 1977, 1995, 2020 by The Lockman Foundation. Used by permission. All rights reserved. lockman.org. Scripture marked with the designation "GW" is taken from GOD'S WORD®. © 1995, 2003, 2013, 2014, 2019, 2020 by God's Word to the Nations Mission Society. Used by permission. Scripture quotations are from the ESV® Bible (The Holy Bible, English Standard Version®), © 2001 by Crossway, a publishing ministry of Good News Publishers. ESV Text Edition: 2025. The ESV text may not be quoted in any publication made available to the public by a Creative Commons license. The ESV may not be translated in whole or in part into any other language. Used by permission. All rights reserved.

ISBN: 978-1-4866-2761-5
eBook ISBN: 978-1-4866-2762-2

Word Alive Press
119 De Baets Street Winnipeg, MB R2J 3R9
www.wordalivepress.ca

Cataloguing in Publication information can be obtained from Library and Archives Canada.

DEDICATION

THIS BOOK IS dedicated to the memory of a great man of God, Melvin Paulus. He was born on January 23, 1935 and went to be with the Lord on December 15, 2022. His ministry began when he was seventeen years old and he went on to preach the gospel for fifty-five years as a pastor and traveling evangelist, from 1952 to 2007. He still preached the gospel at times when he was in his eighties.

His love for Jesus was real and easily seen by the way he loved everyone around him.

That love had its impact on me early in 1968, just before I turned eighteen, when Melvin held revival meetings at our church. My life was a broken mess. I had no hope or any awareness of God's love. Anger drove most of my actions. But I went to a meeting one evening to listen to him speak, trying not to look at him as he spoke. Every word stirred my heart and made me hungry for the reality of Jesus.

At the end of the service, he invited anyone who wanted to find peace with God to come to the front. I went stumbling and crying, broken and looking for hope. Later, Melvin and I spoke in the basement of the church. He listened to my questions and then shared the love of Jesus without looking at the clock. Around midnight, we went home.

The next morning, my room was full of the peace and love of Jesus. All the anger was gone and I felt the presence of something greater than I had ever known.

If I could say something to Melvin today, it would be simply this: "Thank you for sharing Jesus with me!"

INTRODUCTION

THIS DEVOTIONAL IS written for anyone who's interested in discovering the beauty and perfection of God's words, spoken since time began, to many different people in many different situations.

When God speaks, His words are perfect and always accomplish their purpose. At times they have been explosive, immediately effective, and seen by all. Other times they are quiet and only noticed by a few. Not everyone who hears His words responds the same way. Some embrace them while others totally reject them. Our reactions to God and opinions of His words have nothing to do with our knowledge or intellectual capacity; our response is driven by the heart.

The Bible identifies the utterances of God in many ways. In the New Testament era, the words of God, written down by the prophets, are referred to as "scripture." They treated scripture as a holy writ, God's words written down and preserved. Scripture was carefully guarded and highly respected because it was considered sacred.

However, the power of God's words wasn't found in the lives of those who honoured the sacred writings without honouring the One from whom those writings came. Such people crucified the living Word, the only One who had perfectly lived out every word God ever spoke.

LIGHT DECLARES WHO GOD IS

> The earth was formless and empty, and darkness covered the deep water. The Spirit of God was hovering over the water.
> Then God said, "Let there be light!" So there was light. God saw the light was good. So God separated the light from the darkness. God named the light day, and the darkness he named night. There was evening, then morning—the first day. (Genesis 1:2–5, GW)

THE SPIRIT OF God was hovering over the water at the same time as the darkness. Only darkness was visible, appearing as an empty, worthless ruin. But God was there. It would be impossible to know how long this condition existed because there was no time.

However, it all changed in an instant.

God was moving, fluttering unseen over the deep water. Then He spoke four words that changed the world: *"Let there be light!"* The result of those words was guaranteed: *"So there was light."* The light didn't eliminate the darkness, but it separated light from darkness. Light was needed so the beauty of God's work could be seen. Darkness would no longer hide it.

The presence of light begins a beautiful change in our lives as well, just as it did at the time of creation.

> This is the message we heard from Christ and are reporting to you: God is light, and there isn't any darkness in him. If we say, "We have a relationship

with God" and yet live in the dark, we're lying. We aren't being truthful. (1 John 1:5–6, GW)

Light makes it possible to see, as well as to be seen. Light first came into my darkness when I was seventeen years old, illuminating my path and destiny. My life didn't look good.

The light also shone brightly on the path God was making available to me. This path looked so inviting and peaceful. The presence of Jesus was there, and I knew He saw me.

That light appeared to me, like it has for so many others, because of those four words God spoke, *"Let there be light!"* Darkness could no longer hide God's beauty, which is seen in the light not just because of what He is doing but because of who He is. God *is* light.

> You belong to the day and the light not to the night and the dark. Therefore, we must not fall asleep like other people, but we must stay awake and be sober.
> (1 Thessalonians 5:5–6, GW)

At times, life will seem dark and our faith will be tested. It may even seem like all hope is lost, never to return. During these times, our captivation of the light will hold us steady because we know that the morning light will appear, bringing joy with it. Morning will always come because God said, *"Let there be light!"*

SEPARATION OF ABOVE AND BELOW

Then God said, "Let there be a horizon in the middle of the water in order to separate the water." So God made the horizon and separated the water above and below the horizon. And so it was. God named what was above the horizon sky. There was evening, then morning—a second day. (Genesis 1:6–8, GW)

GOD MADE THE horizon by the active power of His words. He not only made it but gave it purpose. It was to be a dividing line between everything in the sky and everything on earth. The earth was still covered with water at this time. The water below the horizon was physical, occupying space and held in place by gravity. The water above the horizon was contained in the air, unseen; we would know it as humidity.

Despite the differences between the two waters, God used both in a beautiful way to help us to better recognize Him and understand how different His ways are from ours.

God expressed His life through words, thus separating light from darkness and water above from water below. He changed the physical world one day at a time. Living in light was nothing like living in the dark, and neither was living above the horizon anything like living below it.

One day, Jesus spoke to a Samaritan woman beside a well. She had come to fill her jugs with water and be on her way, but Jesus introduced her to a different kind of water. It was the heavenly kind, one that had a completely different impact than the water with which she was filling her jugs. The water she drew from the earth would leave her thirsty again, but the water from above, offered by Jesus, would satisfy eternally. It was available simply because God said so.

> Jesus replied, "Anyone who drinks this water will soon become thirsty again. But those who drink the water I give will never be thirsty again. It becomes a fresh, bubbling spring within them, giving them eternal life." (John 4:13–14, NLT)

God made the horizon so we could perceive the dividing line, separating what's above from what's below. Just as the waters are different on opposite sides of the horizon, so is the life lived in each part.

Living above the horizon isn't complicated. You won't achieve it through excessive strength or self-discipline. The only way to live there is to be hidden in Christ, with your eyes set on the eternal realities above the horizon, not on the temporary issues below it.

God spoke and created the horizon. Will I spend my life above it or below it?

Day Three
LET THE EARTH PRODUCE

Then God said, "Let the water under the sky come together in one area, and let the dry land appear." And so it was. God named the dry land earth. The water which came together he named sea. God saw that it was good. Then God said, "Let the earth produce vegetation: plants bearing seeds, each according to its own type, and fruit trees bearing fruit with seeds, each according to its own type." And so it was. The earth produced vegetation: plants bearing seeds, each according to its own type, and trees bearing fruit with seeds, each according to its own type. God saw that they were good. There was evening, then morning—a third day. (Genesis 1:9–13, GW)

THE WORDS GOD spoke on the third day set a perfect process in motion. First, He needed to prepare a place for vegetation and fruit-bearing trees. These trees and vegetation were then given the ability to grow and reproduce year after year, just because God said that's the way it would be. These plants could only reproduce according to their own kind, though, regardless of which other plants may have been nearby.

Today we have all kinds of hybrid seeds that have been produced by crosspollination. But when these plants are left alone, they go back to producing their original seeds, because that's how God said it would be. This is how they fulfill their purpose.

David saw this over and over again as he led his sheep to the green pastures:

> He causeth the grass to grow for the cattle, and herb for the service of man: that he may bring forth food out of the earth… (Psalm 104:14, KJV)

In His wisdom, God knew what it would take to create an earth that would produce sustainable life. All He had to do then was to use His words, speaking it into being. The earth heard and responded—and the earth is still responding today.

If the earth hears and responds to His words, what will my life be like when I hear and respond?

Day Four
THE PURPOSE OF LIGHTS

Then God said, "Let there be lights in the sky to separate the day from the night. They will be signs and will mark religious festivals, days, and years. They will be lights in the sky to shine on the earth." And so it was. God made the two bright lights: the larger light to rule the day and the smaller light to rule the night. He also made the stars. God put them in the sky to give light to the earth, to dominate the day and the night, and to separate the light from the darkness. God saw that it was good. There was evening, then morning—a fourth day. (Genesis 1:14–19, GW)

CAN YOU IMAGINE a world without the sun, moon, or stars? In the early days of creation, it was simply light or dark. There was no sunrise or sunset, and the night contained no moonlight or starlight. There would have been no ocean tides. Neither were there distinct seasons.

Then God spoke once again! His words produced the lights in the sky. He then gave them each a purpose, one which they continue to fulfill. He created a large light to dominate the day, and a lesser light to dominate the night. The simple words of God brought these amazing lights into being.

The shepherd David probably spent many days and nights on the hillsides caring for his sheep. He would have been very aware of the beauty of his surroundings, as well as the presence of God. He wrote about it in the psalms:

Both the day and the night are yours; you made the sun and the moon. You set all the limits on the earth; you created summer and winter. (Psalm 74:16–17, NCV)

Our lives contain many different seasons, just as in creation. There are times when the light shines brightly, but also times when the darkness feels almost suffocating. God knew it would be this way. His words declared it. But He didn't stop speaking.

I can rest whether I'm experiencing a time of illumination or darkness because God's word created a light to rule in both conditions.

Day Five

HE FILLS EVERYTHING

> Then God said, "Let the water swarm with swimming creatures, and let birds fly through the sky over the earth." So God created the large sea creatures, every type of creature that swims around in the water and every type of flying bird. God saw that they were good. God blessed them and said, "Be fertile, increase in number, fill the sea, and let there be many birds on the earth." There was evening, then morning—a fifth day. (Genesis 1:20–23, GW)

GOD NEVER PLANNED to leave creation empty and neglected. His intentions were always for the earth to have more than just sunrises and sunsets, even though they are beautiful. He wanted it to be filled with life that moved and reproduced. Some of that life would fly, some would walk, and some would swim. All these actions are different, but they display God's beauty.

The words God used to speak all these creatures into being did more than make them beautiful. His words also gave them limits, and those limits were part of their unique beauty, separating themselves one from another.

God—who is complete, unlimited, and needs nothing—was preparing a place for man, who would be limited and needy, just like the rest of creation. God didn't need this man, but this man would surely need God.

> Lord, you have made many things; with your wisdom you made them all. The earth is full of your riches.

Look at the sea, so big and wide, with creatures large and small that cannot be counted. Ships travel over the ocean, and there is the sea monster Leviathan, which you made to play there. All these things depend on you to give them their food at the right time. When you give it to them, they gather it up. When you open your hand, they are filled with good food. When you turn away from them, they become frightened. When you take away their breath, they die and turn to dust. When you breathe on them, they are created, and you make the land new again. (Psalm 104:24–30, NCV)

We are honoured to see the beauty created by the words of God, and to see the care that God gives every part of it. All creation is dependent on God.

HE CREATED MAN IN HIS OWN IMAGE

Then God said, "Let the earth produce every type of living creature: every type of domestic animal, crawling animal, and wild animal." And so it was. God made every type of wild animal, every type of domestic animal, and every type of creature that crawls on the ground. God saw that they were good.

Then God said, "Let us make humans in our image, in our likeness. Let them rule the fish in the sea, the birds in the sky, the domestic animals all over the earth, and all the animals that crawl on the earth."

So God created humans in his image. In the image of God he created them. He created them male and female.

God blessed them and said, "Be fertile, increase in number, fill the earth, and be its master. Rule the fish in the sea, the birds in the sky, and all the animals that crawl on the earth."

God said, "I have given you every plant with seeds on the face of the earth and every tree that has fruit with seeds. This will be your food. I have given all green plants as food to every land animal, every bird in the sky, and every animal that crawls on the earth—every living, breathing animal." And so it was.

And God saw everything that he had made and that it was very good. There was evening, then morning—the sixth day. (Genesis 1:24–31, GW)

AFTER GOD HAD spoken and made all the creatures that walked the ground, he had one thing left to do that day. Needing a caretaker, he made humans, and he made them male and female so they could multiply and manage everything else God had made, just as all of creation was now multiplying and filling the earth.

The process of creating humans sounds similar to the way in which God made everything else. God said, and then it happened.

However, God performed another act while creating humans. This was something He didn't do regarding any other aspect of creation.

> And the Lord God formed man of the dust of the ground, and breathed into his nostrils the breath of life; and man became a living soul. (Genesis 2:7, KJV)

He took dust from the dry land, the land which He had separated from the water, and gave that dust a shape by squeezing it as a potter works clay. When it was shaped and had a face, God breathed into it and gave it life. That life came from the breath of God; the man wasn't just the result of God's declaration. This set humanity apart from everything else God made.

This is a good lesson for us. Once we have seen God do something, we very easily think we know God's ways and assume He will always repeat His actions. While all of God's ways are perfect (2 Samuel 22:31), though, we cannot assume that they are predictable.

Day Seven
GETTING OUR ATTENTION

One day Moses was tending the flock of his father-in-law, Jethro, the priest of Midian. He led the flock far into the wilderness and came to Sinai, the mountain of God. There the angel of the Lord appeared to him in a blazing fire from the middle of a bush. Moses stared in amazement. Though the bush was engulfed in flames, it didn't burn up. "This is amazing," Moses said to himself. "Why isn't that bush burning up? I must go see it."

When the Lord saw Moses coming to take a closer look, God called to him from the middle of the bush, "Moses! Moses!"

"Here I am!" Moses replied.

"Do not come any closer," the Lord warned. "Take off your sandals, for you are standing on holy ground. I am the God of your father—the God of Abraham, the God of Isaac, and the God of Jacob."

When Moses heard this, he covered his face because he was afraid to look at God. (Exodus 3:1–6, NLT)

GOD INTENDS FOR us to clearly hear when He speaks. The occasion may not always be marked by a big dramatic event, but we won't be able to forget the impact of God speaking His words directly to us.

Moses's encounter with God totally changed the course of his life. He had left a life of luxury in Pharaoh's house forty years earlier to take care of sheep in the desert. The last thing he expected was a visitation from God. I don't know how many times Moses walked through this particular area where the encounter happened, but nothing had ever happened before. Then God spoke and told him to take off his shoes, for he was standing on holy ground.

Imagine the context. For forty years, he had walked the desert, caring for sheep. That's about fourteen thousand six hundred days. Why would anyone expect God to show up suddenly and start speaking? There must have been a significant reason to free Moses from this deadly condition of living with no expectation.

The same is true for us.

God got Moses's attention perfectly, lighting a little fire in a bush. Except the bush didn't burn up and turn to ash. Noticing this detail, Moses changed up his routine. No doubt he said to himself, *I must go and see this.*

There is something uniquely compelling and purposeful about God moving to get our attention. And when He speaks, we have no doubt about who is talking and who should listen. His words reshape our hearts, permanently altering the course of our lives.

The living words of God are not found in dead letters written on the pages of a book; they come to us when we encounter Him and hear His voice. Our changed lives are proof that we have heard Him speak.

Day Eight
RESPONDING TO THE UNEXPECTED PRESENCE

> Joshua was near Jericho when he looked up and saw a man standing in front of him with a sword in his hand. Joshua went to him and asked, "Are you a friend or an enemy?"
>
> The man answered, "I am neither. I have come as the commander of the Lord's army."
>
> Then Joshua bowed facedown on the ground and asked, "Does my master have a command for me, his servant?"
>
> The commander of the Lord's army answered, "Take off your sandals, because the place where you are standing is holy." So Joshua did. (Joshua 5:13–15, NCV)

ON A DAY of new beginnings for Israel, the people arrived in the land God had promised them. They enjoyed the Passover feast and began eating food they had grown. They no longer needed manna.

As they got ready to conquer the cities of this new land, Joshua looked around. He was probably wondering how to defeat the well-fortified city of Jericho. I imagine him standing on an overlook, deep in thought, when something caused him to glance up. There in front of him stood a man with a sword in hand. Joshua responded like any good leader, unafraid of the conflict before him.

"Are you a friend or an enemy?" Joshua challenged, ready to respond to either response. It was a this-or-that kind of question, with only two possible answers.

This is often the mindset of knowledgeable and confident leaders. They view life through a lens that dims weakness and brightens strength, leaving little room for anything else.

In this moment, Joshua had an encounter with the One who knows everything, because He is everything.

When we find ourselves in a circumstance like that, we need to have an attitude that says "He knows and I don't. He is and I am not." That's the only attitude that results in the correct action.

As soon as Joshua became aware of this man's identity, he understood and responded in the correct way. He no longer felt the need to give orders; he instead desired to take orders.

The top commander of the Lord's army not only gave Joshua a command, He also gave the reason for it, because there was no time for Joshua to ask, "Why?" Just as with Moses, Joshua was told to take off his shoes, because he stood on holy ground. This ground implies so much more than a physical location; it also includes the condition of one's mind.

In this place, and in this condition, God gave Joshua the full instructions for defeating Jericho. If we keep our internal condition clean, knowing that we are to consider this condition holy, we will always be at the right place at the right time to hear God's instructions for us to live victoriously.

Day Nine
PERFECTLY DECLARED INSTRUCTIONS

Jericho was bolted and barred shut because the people were afraid of the Israelites. No one could enter or leave.

The Lord said to Joshua, "I am about to hand Jericho, its king, and its warriors over to you. All the soldiers will march around the city once a day for six days. Seven priests will carry rams' horns ahead of the ark. But on the seventh day you must march around the city seven times while the priests blow their horns. When you hear a long blast on the horn, all the troops must shout very loudly. The wall around the city will collapse. Then the troops must charge straight ahead into the city." (Joshua 6:1–5, GW)

GETTING INSIDE THE walls of Jericho wouldn't be a simple feat. The walls were very thick. In fact, they were so thick that houses had been built on top of them. When the gates in these walls were locked, nobody could go in or out. If you were outside, you were locked out; if you were inside, you were locked in. The city's officials had maintained this control for many years, and it had always worked well for them.

That is, until the Lord showed up and gave some very unusual instructions to His servant Joshua. These detailed instructions would change the world for those in Jericho, as well as for Israel, as long as the instructions were perfectly followed.

How often might our own worlds be changed, whether this involves getting outside the walls that lock us in or getting into places we're locked out of? Israel spent forty years traveling through the desert to reach the place God had promised them.

The walled city of Jericho must have looked like an impossible target, like so many difficult situations in our lives. The sight of those high, thick walls didn't stop the Israelites.

They did, however, wait.

There's a difference between *stopping* and *waiting*. When I stop being involved in a situation, it's like parking my car, getting out of the vehicle, and leaving. But when I'm in a period of waiting, I stay inside the parked car, ready to move again at the right time.

The moment I stop waiting is when I receive what I need to get moving again.

The greatest motivation to get moving again is the voice of God bringing us detailed instructions on how to move forward. The proverbial walls are no longer an issue, because we hear and recognize His wisdom.

His words are just as real and powerful today. He speaks to us while we wait, just as He spoke to Joshua. We must have the same attitude that Joshua had.

After Joshua declared himself a servant of God, he received divine instructions. These instructions were pretty safe to follow, except the last one: *"Then the troops must charge straight ahead into the city."*

They did it, and they won. Let's do the same!

Day Ten
THE WORD REFINED HIM

> He sent a man before them, even Joseph, who was sold for a servant: whose feet they hurt with fetters: he was laid in iron: until the time that his word came: the word of the Lord tried him. The king sent and loosed him; even the ruler of the people, and let him go free. He made him lord of his house, and ruler of all his substance: to bind his princes at his pleasure; and teach his senators wisdom. (Psalm 105:17–22, KJV)

JOSEPH HAD A very unusual life. He was probably a bit pampered since he was his father's favourite child. This produced some tension in the family and his brothers hated him.

This didn't keep God from setting His heart on this child, even if he did feel a bit entitled.

When a person grows up with a sense of entitlement, they have few good relational connections. Their own sense of specialness makes it impossible for them to recognize that someone else may have needs. As a result, they never step in and help.

Even though this describes Joseph, God gave him accurate dreams of the future. All Joseph could see from these dreams was that everyone and everything bowed down to him. He had no idea of the process it would take for any of this to actually happen. His brothers hated him because Joseph thought his brothers should *already* be bowing to him. If only he had known what was to happen, he may not have revealed those dreams so quickly.

His circumstances quickly changed when he became a slave. This was the opposite of everything he had previously known. But something inside Joseph compelled him to serve Potifar, the captain of the guard in Pharaoh's army, and he served with his whole heart.

God was with him. It's evident that He had blessed the house of Potifar. God was blessing Joseph too, the evidence of which is seen in what happened after a false accusation sent him to prison. Joseph remained faithful and was able to see things he had never seen before.

> But the Lord was with Joseph, and shewed him mercy… (Genesis 39:21, KJV)

During this dark time, Joseph discovered mercy. This word of truth gave him the capacity to extend mercy to his brothers, breaking the power of the shackles that held his body. More than that, mercy purified his heart so perfectly that God could trust him while others bowed to him.

The word of the Lord will purify your heart during difficult experiences, especially when you discover mercy.

Day Eleven
BRIGHT AND UNCONTAMINATED WORDS

> The words of the Lord are pure words: as silver tried in a furnace of earth, purified seven times. Thou shalt keep them, O Lord, thou shalt preserve them from this generation for ever. (Psalm 12:6–7, KJV)
>
> Thy word is very pure: therefore thy servant loveth it. (Psalm 119:140, KJV)
>
> Every word of God is pure: he is a shield unto them that put their trust in him. Add thou not unto his words, lest he reprove thee, and thou be found a liar. (Proverbs 30:5–6, KJV)

DAVID HAD A unique relationship with God and knew Him well. When he made declarations about God, it was all based on his life experience, not speculation or stories he'd heard from others. David knew that every one of God's words is pure—perfectly clean, having been purified like silver, with no chance of ever deteriorating. They could be trusted and would accomplish their purpose.

We should desire to be in that same place David found himself when he declared the pure, powerful beauty of God's words. To get there, we'll need to get acquainted with God in the same way. This will require more than reading about Him in a book or listening to sermons on Sunday morning, because getting acquainted with God has little to do with information or intelligence.

David became acquainted with God during times of isolation on a mountain, defending his sheep from lions and bears. Other times he lived in caves, running from an evil king who wanted to kill him.

Throughout this, David found love for the purity in the word of God, who taught him that it was like a shield, defending him from every evil thing that tried to destroy him.

Our restless lives grow peaceful when we discover the powerful beauty of the pure words spoken to us directly from the mouth of God. Those words alone will be our defence. Our appreciation for them will keep us from polluting scripture by adding our own words. As we read in Proverbs 30, *"Every word of God is pure."*

Day Twelve
PERFECTLY TAUGHT WITH CLEAN WORDS

> The ways of God are without fault. The Lord's words are pure. He is a shield to those who trust him. Who is God? Only the Lord. Who is the Rock? Only our God. God is my protection. He makes my way free from fault. He makes me like a deer that does not stumble; he helps me stand on the steep mountains. He trains my hands for battle so my arms can bend a bronze bow. You protect me with your saving shield. You support me with your right hand. You have stooped to make me great. You give me a better way to live, so I live as you want me to. (Psalm 18:30–36, NCV)

WHAT MADE IT possible for David to say that he lived the way God wanted him to? That's a bold declaration, and one that few people can honestly make. But this kind of life is entirely possible. It's the kind of life Jesus talked about. It's just not often chosen.

> For the gate is narrow and the way is constricted that leads to life, and there are few who find it. (Matthew 7:14, NASB)

This gives us no options from which to pick and choose. The way is set. We don't choose this path for its easy conditions.

I can only make this kind of journey once I'm convinced of two absolute truths.

The first truth: *"The ways of God are without fault."* If I believe this, the quality of my character will protect me from self-pity or complaining when difficulties and injustice disrupt my life. I won't seek an easier path when I'm falsely accused or hated because of my faith, due to the contentment I feel from knowing that God has set my path. This makes the path perfect, and I wouldn't want it any other way.

The second truth: *"The Lord's words are pure."* The only time His words impact me is when I seek the path that's free and clean. God will keep His words alive in my heart because of who He is. This was obvious to David, who trusted Him completely. This trust brought David into the Lord's presence. David addressed God directly, in the first person, because the relationship was eye to eye, lived in full view of each other.

If I choose to walk the path with God, it will be pure and clean. If I desire anything that isn't clean, I can't bring it with me along the narrow path. I would instead have to take the path that leads to destruction, where the pure words of God are rejected.

Choose to live the way He wants you to. It's the path that leads to life.

Day Thirteen
HIS WORD LIVES FOREVER

Now that your obedience to the truth has purified your souls, you can have true love for your Christian brothers and sisters. So love each other deeply with all your heart. You have been born again, and this new life did not come from something that dies, but from something that cannot die. You were born again through God's living message that continues forever. The Scripture says,

"All people are like the grass, and all their glory is like the flowers of the field. The grass dies and the flowers fall, but the word of the Lord will live forever." And this is the word that was preached to you. (1 Peter 1:22–25, NCV)

SHARING LOVE WITH the people around us produces a healthy atmosphere of safety. It's safe because these relationships are permanently anchored in a life made clean through obedience and a commitment to truth.

Christians too often claim to be clean based entirely on what Jesus did, failing to participate in the process, except for expressing a belief in Jesus as Saviour. This expression of faith is an important step, but it only takes a person partway. To get the benefit of what Jesus did, we must walk with Him.

> But if we walk in the light, as he is in the light, we have fellowship one with another, and the blood of Jesus Christ his Son cleanseth us from all sin. (1 John 1:7, KJV)

In this verse, the words *"but if"* are significant. If I want His cleanness, I must do more than believe in the principles He lived for; I must actually live His life. If I don't, I'll be like a patch of grass that dies, or a flower that fades, no longer having any beauty.

Those who have truly been born again and walk in the light never die, because their lives come from He who cannot die. They remain clean because of the work of the blood of Jesus, which wasn't a one-time event. That work is current and continuous, rooted in the eternal truth of God found in one of the most popular verses in the Bible: *"For God so loved the world, that he gave..."* (John 3:16, KJV)

The nature of our eternal God is *love*, and that love motivates Him to *give*. The same is true for us. When His eternal word is alive in us, we are motivated to give to others because we love Him, rather than those who take from others because they only love themselves.

When my motivation comes from eternal life, I'll live my whole week the same way I live on Sunday. I'll be at peace with God because of the power of the word He speaks.

Day Fourteen
MOTIVATED BY COMMANDMENTS OR HIS WORD

> Here's how we can be sure that we know God in the right way: Keep his commandments.
> If someone claims, "I know him well!" but doesn't keep his commandments, he's obviously a liar. His life doesn't match his words. But the one who keeps God's word is the person in whom we see God's mature love. This is the only way to be sure we're in God. Anyone who claims to be intimate with God ought to live the same kind of life Jesus lived. (1 John 2:2–6, MSG)

THERE'S SOMETHING IMPRESSIVE about the detailed commands God has given. This study of them gives us a good picture of the actions of which God approves, and those He doesn't. While it's important to understand which behaviours God expects of us, this knowledge only gives us a safe shell in which to live. The shell itself has no life. At best, it reveals that I know something about God and respect His directives.

The fear of being punished for disobedience strongly motivates us when all we know about God is His commands. This fear is what gives legalistic religion its strength, painting an incomplete picture of God. It lacks the intimacy of seeing and touching Him.

> We write you now about what has always existed, which we have heard, we have seen with our own eyes, we have looked at, and we have touched with

our hands. We write to you about the Word that gives life. (1 John 1:1, NCV)

The difference between the commands of God and the word of God is very simple. The commands alone are dead facts; the word is a living expression. We usually learn the facts first, and those facts can stimulate us to make adjustments in our lives. John wrote about *"what has always existed, which we have heard..."* I can almost hear the excitement in his voice as he adds that *"we have seen with our own eyes, we have looked at, and we have touched with our hands."*

Before Jesus, the disciples lived their lives with God's commands and promises dictating their daily activities. When Jesus came, they lived with Him, watched Him, and touched Him. This went on for more than three years, during which time He showed them the beauty of going beyond the commandments in order to live relationally with God Himself.

On the day of Pentecost, it all came together and they intimately saw, touched with their own hands, and felt God's presence. In that moment, they became motivated based on God's expression of love, rather than merely the commandments themselves. Their relationship with God changed. God's love changed their world, and it will change ours too when we intimately see and touch Him.

Day Fifteen
NO LONGER JACOB

When the man saw that he could not win against Jacob, he touched the socket of Jacob's hip so that it was dislocated as they wrestled. Then the man said, "Let me go; it's almost dawn."

But Jacob answered, "I won't let you go until you bless me."

So the man asked him, "What's your name?"

"Jacob," he answered.

The man said, "Your name will no longer be Jacob but Israel [He Struggles With God], because you have struggled with God and with men—and you have won."

Jacob said, "Please tell me your name."

The man answered, "Why do you ask for my name?" Then he blessed Jacob there. So Jacob named that place Peniel [Face of God], because he said, "I have seen God face to face, but my life was saved." The sun rose as he passed Penuel. He was limping because of his hip. (Genesis 32:25–31, GW)

JACOB WAS A very intense man whose actions clearly defined him. He wasn't content to be lesser than anyone else. In fact, he did everything he could to get ahead of those who seemed to have an advantage over him. He was willing to lie, cheat, and steal to gain an advantage.

Ultimately he paid a high price for his actions. He produced a lot of tension in his family and he lost many familiar relationships.

Then a word from God changed everything, beginning with an urge he felt to return to his homeland and reconnect with his brother Esau. He had to be aware that this might not go well, since Esau had vowed to kill him as soon as their father died.

So Jacob carefully planned his return, knowing that God had promised to be with him. He organized every detail, expecting his plans to accomplish what he wanted. What he didn't know was how it would all work out.

But God did. Jacob wasn't in charge. God was.

When a host of angels showed up (Genesis 32:1–2), Jacob should have known that something very significant was about to happen—and it happened later that same night as he wrestled with God.

The words God spoke during this encounter resulted in a change of name, better revealing his eternal nature; from that time forward, he was called Israel. And the touch that came with the encounter changed him externally; for the rest of his life, he walked with a limp.

It's better to have a limp and struggle *with* God than it is to be free of limits and yet struggle *against* God.

Day Sixteen
HIS WORDS ARE VERY NEAR

This command I'm giving you today isn't too hard for you or beyond your reach. It's not in heaven. You don't have to ask, "Who will go to heaven to get this command for us so that we can hear it and obey it?" This command isn't on the other side of the sea. You don't have to ask, "Who will cross the sea to get it for us so that we can hear it and obey it?" No, these words are very near you. They're in your mouth and in your heart so that you will obey them.

Today I offer you life and prosperity or death and destruction. This is what I'm commanding you today: Love the Lord your God, follow his directions, and obey his commands, laws, and rules. Then you will live, your population will increase, and the Lord your God will bless you in the land that you're about to enter and take possession of. (Deuteronomy 30:11–16, GW)

THIS PASSAGE SHOWS God speaking to Israel just before they took possession of the Promised Land. They had experienced many encounters with God in the past forty years. Some had been wonderful while others were devastating. They often misunderstood what God was trying to tell them. Other times, they simply rejected His advice.

As a result, they missed out on the benefit God intended to give them. They concluded that since they weren't seeing much benefit, it was probably because the fulfilment of God's promise was either still a long way off or too complicated. They didn't believe it was possible for the benefit to be as close and relevant as it was.

God wanted to change their perspective so they would know Him in a physically close way, with Him being involved in their activities. He wanted to have a relationship with each of them personally, as well as with the nation as a whole, so that He could speak and they could relate both individually and corporately. He wanted them to know the powerful influence of His words being placed in their hearts, causing them to not just clearly speak God's words but also immediately respond.

God's desire is the same towards us today. The words He speaks to us aren't locked up in the distant past, nor are they some hidden mystery of the future that we have to puzzle out.

> Men and brethren, children of the stock of Abraham, and whosoever among you feareth God, to you is the word of this salvation sent. (Acts 13:26, KJV)

God is just as alive today as He was when He spoke to Israel. The power of His words hasn't changed. His intention is for His words to have such a place in our hearts that they affect every expression of our lives as we love Him with our whole hearts, living as He directs us.

Day Seventeen
THE BENEFIT OF CONTROLLING MY MOUTH

> You have tested my heart; You have visited me in the night; You have tried me and have found nothing; I have purposed that my mouth shall not transgress. Concerning the works of men, by the word of Your lips, I have kept away from the paths of the destroyer. Uphold my steps in Your paths, that my footsteps may not slip.
>
> I have called upon You, for You will hear me, O God; incline Your ear to me, and hear my speech. (Psalm 17:3–6, NKJV)

DAVID WAS A great man and successful at relating to God, even though he made some mistakes along the way. But his great relationship with God was his salvation many times. He knew how to faithfully follow his Good Shepherd. Amazingly, it wasn't all that complicated, though it would be difficult to achieve without a deliberate plan. It all centred around his mouth.

During difficult times, David knew God was putting him to the test. When these tests were finished, he could declare that there was no wrong found in him. He knew he had passed, and he knew the reason why: *"I have purposed that my mouth shall not transgress."* He kept his speech within God's boundaries to best hear Him without interruption.

Have you ever watched two people engaged in intense conversation interrupt and talk over each other? David didn't want to do that with God. He kept himself off the path of destruction by the power of God's words. And when David called out to God for help, he knew God would respond.

David was more of a listener than a talker: *"Set a watch, O Lord, before my mouth; keep the door of my lips"* (Psalm 141:3, KJV). Could it be that the overuse of our own mouths causes us to minimize the power and beauty of God's words? As Proverbs 13:3 states, *"Those who control their tongue will have a long life; opening your mouth can ruin everything"* (NLT).

Day Eighteen
UNABLE TO HEAR AND FOLLOW INSTRUCTIONS

"The time is surely coming," says the Sovereign Lord, "when I will send a famine on the land—not a famine of bread or water but of hearing the words of the Lord. People will stagger from sea to sea and wander from border to border searching for the word of the Lord, but they will not find it. Beautiful girls and strong young men will grow faint in that day, thirsting for the Lord's word. And those who swear by the shameful idols of Samaria—who take oaths in the name of the god of Dan and make vows in the name of the god of Beersheba—they will all fall down, never to rise again." (Amos 8:11–14, NLT)

A FAMINE CAN be defined in many ways, but it most often results in the most severe hunger crises. Large numbers of people die from starvation during a famine. They're not normally caused by one event or condition. Several devastating occurrences often dovetail to create them.

When God spoke to the prophet Amos, He could see the nation of Israel's direction. *"I will send a famine,"* He said, and it wasn't an isolated event. This fame would come because of several conditions under which Israel had chosen to dwell.

None of this would end well.

The famine was of a spiritual type, preventing the people from *"hearing the words of the Lord."* It's not that God's words weren't available; rather, they couldn't hear them. All of God's words are true and active from the moment they are spoken, and they remain that way forever. Nothing can change them but God Himself, if He chooses to.

> Thy word is true from the beginning: and every one of thy righteous judgments [declarations] endureth for ever. (Psalm 119:160, KJV)

This famine was all about hearing. Why? Were the people becoming deaf? Did they cover their ears because they didn't want to hear Him? Or was it that their chaotic lives, filled with the confusing noise of their own arrogant words, made it impossible for them to hear the gentle words of God? There were probably many reasons.

Let's learn the lessons and avoid the same problem today. The answer is simple. We must say, "God knows, and I don't. His words are eternal; mine aren't." And finally: *"Don't be in a hurry to talk. Don't be eager to speak in the presence of God. Since God is in heaven and you are on earth, limit the number of your words"* (Ecclesiastes 5:2, GW).

Day Nineteen
AGREEMENT WITHOUT COMMITMENT

> And Moses alone shall come near the Lord, but they shall not come near; nor shall the people go up with him.
>
> So Moses came and told the people all the words of the Lord and all the judgments. And all the people answered with one voice and said, "All the words which the Lord has said we will do." And Moses wrote all the words of the Lord. And he rose early in the morning, and built an altar at the foot of the mountain... (Exodus 24:2–4, NKJV)

THE OLD TESTAMENT contains many accounts of Israel responding to God's words. When they obeyed, they enjoyed great and miraculous results. On the other hand, when they rejected Him, the results were tragic.

Thankfully, many of these events were written down so we can learn from them and not repeat them.

> Everything that was written in the past was written to teach us. (Romans 15:4, NCV)

Sometimes we receive the words of God directly. At other times, we receive them through a messenger, as Israel did when Moses gave the people God's words.

No matter how these words come, they are God's words and must be honoured. The issue isn't really about how His words come to us. Rather, how we respond determines the final outcome.

Israel heard His words and could see the benefit for themselves, so they agreed to do everything God said. But when Moses didn't show up as expected, they easily set aside their agreement and made other arrangements, hoping to satisfy their emptiness.

> They have turned aside quickly out of the way which I commanded them. They have made themselves a molded calf, and worshiped it and sacrificed to it, and said, "This is your god, O Israel, that brought you out of the land of Egypt!" (Exodus 32:8, NKJV)

Thousands died because of their actions. They lacked commitment, which would have carried them through unexpected disappointments and given them the ability to continue doing what they had agreed to.

As believers, our world is much like theirs. God gives us words to direct us. At times we hear His voice directly. Other times it's indirect. But no matter how they come, we must deal correctly with Him and His words.

We can follow David's example: *"Your word [declarations] I have hidden in my heart, that I might not sin against You"* (Psalm 119:11, NKJV).

When I have firmly secured all the declarations of God in my heart, no external condition will turn me away from my commitment to do all that God declares for me.

Day Twenty
SEEING CHANGES EVERYTHING

All of God's word has proven to be true. He is a shield to those who come to him for protection. Do not add to his words, or he will reprimand you, and you will be found to be a liar. (Proverbs 30:5–6, GW)

Then Job answered the Lord, "I know that you can do everything and that your plans are unstoppable.

"You said, 'Who is this that belittles my advice without having any knowledge about it?' Yes, I have stated things I didn't understand, things too mysterious for me to know.

"You said, 'Listen now, and I will speak. I will ask you, and you will teach me.' I had heard about you with my own ears, but now I have seen you with my own eyes. That is why I take back what I said, and I sit in dust and ashes to show that I am sorry." (Job 42:1–6, GW)

JOB WAS A very wealthy man with great integrity and wisdom, causing him to be regarded as a very influential person. I would expect that he spent time studying and searching for truths that related to deeper matters than everyday life.

God saw what he was doing and took notice, saying, *"No one in the world is like him! He is a man of integrity: He is decent, he fears God, and he stays away from evil"* (Job 1:8, GW). While this didn't give him any special status with God, it put him on a path to eventually *see* God, not just learn about what He'd said.

The result of Job's intent to learn the important declarations of God could be seen by those around him, and it could be written down.

> A man named Job lived in Uz. He was a man of integrity: He was decent, he feared God, and he stayed away from evil… He was the most influential person in the Middle East. (Job 1:1, 3, GW)

Even with this great testimony, there remained a major lack in his life and relationship with God, and it took several devastating and painful experiences to get him to see what was missing.

There couldn't be any shortcut, no quick quiz to get him where he needed to be. The process was long and hard. At times he could have stopped and stepped out of the path God had set him on. His wife advised him to curse God and die, but he had no desire for that.

Eventually, he encountered God along this painful path and everything changed. Seeing God made it possible for him to understand how shallow he'd been, thinking he knew so much simply because he had heard a few things about God.

Day Twenty-One

HEAR IT, HOLD IT, AND BEAR FRUIT

> Now the parable is this: The seed is the word of God. The ones along the path are those who have heard; then the devil comes and takes away the word from their hearts, so that they may not believe and be saved. And the ones on the rock are those who, when they hear the word, receive it with joy. But these have no root; they believe for a while, and in time of testing fall away. And as for what fell among the thorns, they are those who hear, but as they go on their way they are choked by the cares and riches and pleasures of life, and their fruit does not mature. As for that in the good soil, they are those who, hearing the word, hold it fast in an honest and good heart, and bear fruit with patience. (Luke 8:11–15, ESV)

JESUS OFTEN USED parables to teach valuable lessons to His disciples. Just before He explained this parable, He said, *"He who has ears to hear, let him hear"* (Luke 8:8, ESV). It's important for us to learn these lessons well because the truth doesn't change from one generation to another. It's eternal and remains the same.

This parable deals with the word of God, identified here as a seed. That seed gets scattered everywhere so everyone has the opportunity to relate to it. The life I cultivate for myself will determine what happens when I encounter the word being sown in my environment.

The first ones to encounter it had no chance. The devil just came and took the word. It had no effect on them. They stood around, having no desire to go anywhere or do anything.

The ones who encountered the seed on the rock weren't going anywhere either. They were obsessed with anything that gave them significance—and when they saw the significance of the word, they wanted it. But their hard, rigid lives didn't provide soft soil for the word to take root and grow. Therefore, when adversity came, the word lost its significance.

Other seeds fell among the thorns. This describes people whose only focus is seeking pleasure and avoiding pain. In such an environment, God's word couldn't mature.

At last, seed falls on good soil, representing those whose honest and good hearts enable them to hold on to the word, even in great adversity, and bear fruit.

If you want the life-giving power of God's word, listen carefully and keep your life honest and clean.

Day Twenty-Two
THE MOTIVATION TO OBEY

How can a young person live a pure life? By obeying your word. With all my heart I try to obey you. Don't let me break your commands. I have taken your words to heart so I would not sin against you. Lord, you should be praised. Teach me your demands. My lips will tell about all the laws you have spoken. I enjoy living by your rules as people enjoy great riches. I think about your orders and study your ways. I enjoy obeying your demands, and I will not forget your word.

Do good to me, your servant, so I can live, so I can obey your word. (Psalm 119:9–17, NCV)

IN THIS PASSAGE, David asks a question that's relevant to everyone, in every culture and generation. The question is relevant to anyone who desires a life that's transparent and clean.

If this pure life is possible, how can we achieve it?

David's answer worked thousands of years ago, and it still works today. Human nature hasn't changed and uncleanness is just as destructive. Social media and instant gratification are right at our fingertips, but that's not the reason for our problems. I can't blame my uncleanness on others or the ideas they promote.

To shift from the selfish, unclean path and find the clean, transparent path, I will need to change my heart's desires. These desires motivate my choices and drive me to action.

David tells us how to do it: *"By obeying your word."* It sounds very simple and easy! But it will be extremely difficult if we don't know the powerful influence of God's word in our lives.

David found such beautiful power in the words of God. It didn't matter whether the words came in the form of commands, laws, or other rules; they captivated David's attention. The word was so strong in him that he declared *"I enjoy living by your rules"* and *"I enjoy obeying your demands."* His request to God was that he could keep living and obeying God's word. Obviously, God's word had an enjoyable, overpowering influence on David's life.

Throughout our history, ever since the very beginning, uncleanness has been a destructive force. At the same time, the powerful influence of God's word has been a redeeming force for those who see their beauty and find cleanness.

Day Twenty-Three
THE TRAGEDY OF FORGETTING

> Nevertheless He saved them for His name's sake, that He might make His mighty power known. He rebuked the Red Sea also, and it dried up; so He led them through the depths, as through the wilderness. He saved them from the hand of him who hated them, and redeemed them from the hand of the enemy. The waters covered their enemies; there was not one of them left. Then they believed His words; they sang His praise.
>
> They soon forgot His works; they did not wait for His counsel… (Psalm 106:8–13, NKJV)

ALL OF GOD'S actions have a purpose. There is a reason for everything He does. In fact, He oftentimes intends to accomplish multiple objectives.

His main purpose, though, is to show His character and reveal Himself.

The sad reality is that we often misinterpret what God does for us. Our inflated sense of self-importance messes up our view of what happens around us. We inflate our own egos, even when the events of our lives are specifically intended to make God known in our world.

God performed amazing miraculous things for Israel, especially when they were leaving Egypt. After hundreds of years of slavery, God must have seemed a long way off. His words would have seemed hard to believe. After all, if He cared, why had He left His people in slavery, subject to the commanding voices of their masters? Even if one accepted that He did care, it would have seemed that He wasn't strong enough to do anything about the people's condition.

The time finally came when God was ready to move. In order for them to leave Egypt and make their way to the Promised Land, somehow they would have to listen, believe, and obey. God showed Himself to be stronger than the Egyptians, causing Israel to leave with their hands full. Their escape was exciting!

That is, until they came to the Red Sea. It looked like they would all be forced to head back to Egypt.

But then God's power was seen again. His power in action destroyed the Egyptian army, drowning them in the sea while Israel watched. This marked the end of a four-hundred thirty-year period of subjugation.

After seeing all this happen, Israel believed God's words and sang His praises… until they forgot what He had done on their behalf.

Day Twenty-Four
HIS WORDS GIVE LIFE

He took away your pride when he let you get hungry, and then he fed you with manna, which neither you nor your ancestors had ever seen. This was to teach you that a person does not live on bread alone, but by everything the Lord says. (Deuteronomy 8:3, NCV)

The devil came to Jesus to tempt him, saying, "If you are the Son of God, tell these rocks to become bread."

Jesus answered, "It is written in the Scriptures, 'A person lives not on bread alone, but by everything God says.'" (Matthew 4:3–4, NCV)

IMPORTANT LESSONS ARE best learned through experience. The people of Israel were probably a lot like us, with just enough entitlement to make them think they should never have to go hungry. Going hungry was bad enough. But when they did begin to eat again, they had to eat manna, which fell far below their standard.

God had a purpose for this. He needed to humble them so their pride wouldn't be the driving force, directing their every decision. They were accustomed to manmade food, but God gave them unfamiliar food made by Him.

When Jesus completed His forty days in the wilderness, He was hungry too. The devil came and made a suggestion: Jesus could turn stones into bread because of who He was. He tried to get Jesus to feel entitled as the Son of God. Jesus neither denied this or claimed it. He just brought it into the proper perspective by pointing out the truth.

The truth Jesus presented to Satan is still true today. It's not about claiming rights or entitlements, trying to fill the empty places in our lives. We need to recognize that entitlement doesn't give us life.

God's word brings us provision for life. All that's required of us is to make Him Lord and listen to His desires rather than our own.

Day Twenty-Five
LISTEN AND DO

On the third day there was a wedding in Cana of Galilee, and the mother of Jesus was there; and both Jesus and His disciples were invited to the wedding. When the wine ran out, the mother of Jesus said to Him, "They have no wine."

And Jesus said to her, "What business do you have with Me, woman? My hour has not yet come."

His mother said to the servants, "Whatever He tells you, do it."

Now there were six stone waterpots standing there for the Jewish custom of purification, containing two or three measures each.

Jesus said to them, "Fill the waterpots with water." So they filled them up to the brim. And He said to them, "Draw some out now and take it to the headwaiter." And they took it to him. (John 2:1–8, NASB)

JESUS WAS GAINING attention and followers. He had just been seen by John the Baptist, who declared him to be the Lamb of God. His followers identified Him as the Messiah and Son of God. Jesus heard all this talk, but it never changed His attitude or the way He lived. His eyes and ears were focused on His Father, not Himself.

> Then said Jesus unto them, When ye have lifted up the Son of man, then shall ye know that I am he, and that I do nothing of myself; but as my Father hath taught me, I speak these things. And he that sent

me is with me: the Father hath not left me alone; for I do always those things that please him. (John 8:28–29, KJV)

Jesus never assumed anything. He never looked to promote Himself or inject Himself into other people's unfortunate situations. While He was aware of the situations around Him, His eyes and ears were trained on His Father.

When His mother pointed out a problem at a wedding, that the party had run out of wine, He embraced this attitude.

Mary was looking for a solution. Maybe He could rush out and quickly buy more?

Jesus saw the problem without rushing to a solution. Without any stress or pressure, He tuned His heart, ears, and eyes to His Father. He was free to hear all the instructions His Father wanted to give Him.

Mary must have been watching Him as He listened, because she then advised the servants to do what He said. That's all it took. The problem was solved. Everyone was amazed at the results.

What would our world be like if we would just do what He says?

Day Twenty-Six
YOU WILL BE A WITNESS

> Now a certain Ananias, a man who was devout by the standard of the Law and well spoken of by all the Jews who lived there, came to me, and standing nearby he said to me, "Brother Saul, receive your sight!" And at that very moment I looked up at him. And he said, "The God of our fathers has appointed you to know His will and to see the Righteous One and to hear a message from His mouth. For you will be a witness for Him to all people of what you have seen and heard. Now why do you delay? Get up and be baptized, and wash away your sins by calling on His name." (Acts 22:12–16, NASB)

AFTER SAUL, WHO was later called Paul, had his encounter with Jesus, he had more questions than answers. All his knowledge of scripture couldn't answer the question he had for Jesus. He had been overpowered and couldn't stand up or make any sense of what had just happened. When he looked around, all he saw was bright light.

Every detail of this encounter was planned and executed by God to change Saul from an educated, arrogant, religious man to a humble servant. And it worked. Saul's life quickly changed.

During this encounter, Saul asked only two questions: *"Who are You, Lord?"* (Acts 22:8, NASB) and *"What shall I do, Lord?"* (Acts 22:10, NASB) When he found out who Jesus was, and what He wanted him to do, he became a new man.

Ananias was the man God used to transition Saul onto his new path, healing his eyes so he could see. He was given a new purpose:

to be a servant, knowing and doing the will of God. He would go forward in life seeing Jesus and hearing what He said.

This qualified him to be a true witness. He wouldn't just *talk* the word of God; he would live it, suffer for it, and die for it. For if we want to *be* something, we must more than *do* something.

There are important times in our lives when we're driven to ask questions, just like Saul. Dark, frustrating, and confusing times often stir up our most intense questions, giving us life-changing answers. When we hear the clarity of God's expectation, hopefully our response will match God's perfect declaration.

Day Twenty-Seven
FIND THE ABILITY TO COMFORT

Comfort, comfort my people, says your God. Speak tenderly to Jerusalem, and cry to her that her warfare is ended, that her iniquity is pardoned, that she has received from the Lord's hand double for all her sins.

A voice cries: "In the wilderness prepare the way of the Lord; make straight in the desert a highway for our God. Every valley shall be lifted up, and every mountain and hill be made low; the uneven ground shall become level, and the rough places a plain. And the glory of the Lord shall be revealed, and all flesh shall see it together, for the mouth of the Lord has spoken." (Isaiah 40:1–5, ESV)

GOD'S WORD WILL never prompt us to do something unless His heart has a desire to see it happen. His words and actions are all prompted by the desires of His heart.

Jesus knew well the priorities of His Father's heart. He knew that *"out of the abundance [surplus] of the heart the mouth speaks"* (Matthew 12:34, ESV), so He listened carefully to what His Father said.

The prophet Isaiah also knew this and carefully reported every word God spoke to him. This was the only way for the people of Israel to know the intense priorities of God's heart. And as God reached out to the prophets, they reached out to others to engage in the work of God as well—to see His purpose accomplished.

It became obvious that God desired for someone to comfort His people, speaking tenderly to them and letting them know that all was well between Him and them. Not just anyone could do this. The people needed to be connected to God's heart, feeling the intensity of His desire and knowing the truth of His words.

Then, in Isaiah 40, a voice declares the wonderful truth. The Bible doesn't tell us who spoke these words, only that the voice was heard.

Seven hundred years later, that voice was identified. It was John the Baptist: *"He said, I am the voice of one crying in the wilderness, Make straight the way of the Lord, as said the prophet Esaias"* (John 1:23, KJV).

John the Baptist declared the arrival of One who would change the world, because the glory of the Lord would be seen by everyone. There would be no question or doubt; the one who declared this word was close enough to God to hear it.

It is well with my soul.

Day Twenty-Eight
THE BEAUTY IN HIS WORDS

Truly, I love your commands more than gold, even the finest gold. Each of your commandments is right. That is why I hate every false way.

Your laws are wonderful. No wonder I obey them! The teaching of your word gives light, so even the simple can understand. I pant with expectation, longing for your commands. Come and show me your mercy, as you do for all who love your name. Guide my steps by your word, so I will not be overcome by evil. Ransom me from the oppression of evil people; then I can obey your commandments. Look upon me with love; teach me your decrees. (Psalm 119:127–135, NLT)

SOMETHING HAPPENED IN David's life to give him a great appreciation for everything God said. It's hard to know exactly what that was, but somehow it was connected to his relationship with the one he called his "shepherd."

While he took care of the sheep in the backcountry, away from home, there must have been days when he didn't see anyone. The only conversation would be what passed from David to the sheep.

But there were conversations happening that no one could hear or even dream of.

Being a shepherd can be hard work. David was responsible for the lives of the sheep, making sure they had grass and water. He also protected them from wild animals. He needed to remain always on alert, watching the sheep and planning ahead so they didn't run out of food.

As he did his job, somehow he found time to sing. He wrote down these songs so we would have them today. He was inspired from his heart. His connection to God must have given him security during periods of silence, as well as during periods of chaos when he had to fight and kill bears and lions (1 Samuel 17:37). After such events, he must have reviewed them in his mind and became aware that God had prompted him to take action. This caused him to trust God in everything, knowing he would be safe.

During this process of life, David gained one hundred percent confidence in God. He trusted his shepherd to lead in a perfectly safe way, keeping and delivering him from his own destructive ways. David learned to treasure every word God spoke. These words brought light that illuminated and attracted him to the right path.

David said, *"Your laws are wonderful. No wonder I obey them!"* May the declarations of God be as beautiful to me as they were to David.

Day Twenty-Nine
LEARNING WHY

> My suffering was good for me, for it taught me to pay attention to your decrees. Your instructions are more valuable to me than millions in gold and silver.
>
> You made me; you created me. Now give me the sense to follow your commands. May all who fear you find in me a cause for joy, for I have put my hope in your word. I know, O Lord, that your regulations are fair; you disciplined me because I needed it. Now let your unfailing love comfort me, just as you promised me, your servant. Surround me with your tender mercies so I may live, for your instructions are my delight. (Psalm 119:71–77, NLT)

WHEN DAVID SAID that his suffering was good for him, he was declaring that a painful experience had brought him down to a lower place than he had ever been before. It wasn't just about the pain; it was about his change in position, becoming a servant.

We would never tell someone that their suffering was good for them. But David referred to his own suffering, not some general experience of suffering. He gained insight and value from these experiences. He learned to pay attention as a servant and appreciate the value of God's instruction.

Paul learned a similar lesson. He called it a thorn in his flesh that made him weak (2 Corinthians 12:7). He prayed and wanted God to take the thorn away, so it wouldn't limit him.

God had another way. He didn't remove the problem, but He did explain the reason for it and Paul understood:

> Each time he [God] said, "My grace is all you need. My power works best in weakness." So now I am glad to boast about my weaknesses, so that the power of Christ can work through me. (2 Corinthians 12:9, NLT)

God's actions and instructions in our lives aren't just for our benefit. David said, *"May all who fear you find in me a cause for joy, for I have put my hope in your word."* He wanted his life to be a testimony of true joy, the kind of joy that doesn't come from having lots of wealth, influence, or strength; it only comes from discovering the beauty of God's words, instructing us in how to serve Him. We do His work the way He wants it done.

When I am delighted with the instructions from God, the results will be seen in my life.

Day Thirty
THE VALUE OF GOD'S TEACHINGS

If I had not loved your teachings, I would have died from my sufferings. I will never forget your orders, because you have given me life by them. I am yours. Save me. I want to obey your orders. Wicked people are waiting to destroy me, but I will think about your rules. Everything I see has its limits, but your commands have none. How I love your teachings! I think about them all day long. Your commands make me wiser than my enemies, because they are mine forever. I am wiser than all my teachers, because I think about your rules. I have more understanding than the elders, because I follow your orders. I have avoided every evil way so I could obey your word. (Psalm 119:92–101, NCV)

DAVID HAD A solid relationship with God, something which was proven in many different situations over a long period of time. We particularly see it in his battle with Goliath. Some people praised him while others belittled him. He had to deal with everything in the pressure of the moment.

David decided to use the simple tools God had already put in his hands, working them in a new way. It worked! The giant fell and the whole nation of Israel was delivered from the Philistines, all because a young man named David had stuck with what he knew worked.

Because of his success and favour, he was noticed and promoted by King Saul.

But David quickly became aware that success and favour don't guarantee continued safety. In fact, he learned that a king's jealousy can lead to death.

While David played his harp, trying to soothe the troubled spirit of Saul, his ear listened intently to God, his shepherd. As he wrote, *"Wicked people are waiting to destroy me..."* That listening ear saved his life when a spear came flying at him. Somehow God made him aware of the danger, otherwise there would have been no way to dodge it.

David took nothing for granted, and neither should we. He didn't focus on protecting himself from the actions of wicked people. Instead he focused on his love for God's teaching, which gave him an appreciation for the unlimited nature of God's word. He became wiser than his enemies and teachers. He was able to understand these things because he followed God's orders.

Intellectual understanding can have value, but it's nothing like the understanding that comes from following God's instructions.

Day Thirty-One
HIS WORD MOTIVATES

> I will worship toward Your holy temple, and praise Your name for Your lovingkindness and Your truth; for You have magnified Your word above all Your name. In the day when I cried out, You answered me, and made me bold with strength in my soul.
>
> All the kings of the earth shall praise You, O Lord, when they hear the words of Your mouth. Yes, they shall sing of the ways of the Lord, for great is the glory of the Lord. Though the Lord is on high, yet He regards the lowly; but the proud He knows from afar. (Psalm 138:2–6, NKJV)

THERE IS A motivation behind everything we do, even the most seemingly insignificant action, and it's valuable to know what these motivations are. When we discover what propels good actions, we should guard them so they remain firm in our lives. But we need to eliminate the motivations that stimulate us to do things that have no value.

David said he was motivated to worship "toward" the place of God. He wasn't just sitting someplace and facing that direction; he actively moved towards it. His hunger drew him toward what he was hungry for. The kindness and trustworthiness of God impressed him so much that he was driven to move towards Him, worshipping Him. In this discovery of God, he declared, *"You have magnified Your word above all Your name."*

David discovered something amazing about God's word from his times of fear and weakness. When he cried out to God, He answered! While David worshipped the supreme God, almighty and creator of everything, He discovered that God will give a word to anyone who asks. His answers may seem so insignificant that we miss the motivating power of them.

When God paid attention and spoke to David, it made him strong with boldness in his difficult situation. And when we are honoured to hear words from the mouth of God, we need to respond. There was nothing magical in God's answer that made David bold. He had to respond with an appropriate action: *"All the kings of the earth shall praise You, O Lord, when they hear the words of Your mouth."*

The powerful effect of hearing comes when we don't limit ourselves. We must respond by actually obeying the directives that come with the words of God. That's when we really see His glory.

Day Thirty-Two
THE TRUST OF A SERVANT

> Lord All-Powerful, the God of Israel, you have said to me, "I will make your family great." So I, your servant, am brave enough to pray to you. Lord God, you are God, and your words are true. And you have promised these good things to me, your servant. Please, bless my family. Let it continue before you always. Lord God, you have said so. With your blessing let my family always be blessed. (2 Samuel 7:27–29, NCV)

NOT EVERYONE SEES God in the same way. This could be because not everyone has the same kind of interactions with Him. The way in which I relate to God will determine how I view His actions, whether those actions are towards me or someone else.

My relationship with Him, not my knowledge about Him, formulates how I respond to everything He says and does. If I relate to God as an all-powerful one who's in control of the universe and everything in it, I'll do nothing to compete with Him. I won't try to direct Him. The actions I take will reflect the things He says that He intends to do.

David knew the God of Israel well enough to easily declare that he knew who was in charge. When talking to God, he identified himself as a servant. He did nothing to try and direct God; he only listened to what God said. These words of God were anchored in David's heart because of his relationship with Him. He was convinced that God would always do what He said.

> God is not a human being, and he will not lie. He is not a human, and he does not change his mind.

> What he says he will do, he does. What he promises,
> he makes come true. (Numbers 23:19, NCV)

Since David was a servant, he always listened before he spoke. Then, with great confidence, he could speak back what God had already spoken. He listened as God told him, *"I will make your family great."* With great courage, because he knew God's words were true, he asked God to make his family great.

Why does our faith weaken? Difficult times cause us to move away from God's presence. We lose sight of Him and the sound of His voice. Then we're left on our own, trying to make God move for us rather than moving ourselves closer to Him where we can hear His words.

Never forget: *"What he promises, he makes come true."*

Day Thirty-Three
WHEN JESUS SPOKE

If anyone hears My teachings and does not keep them, I do not judge him; for I did not come to judge the world, but to save the world. The one who rejects Me and does not accept My teachings has one who judges him: the word which I spoke. That will judge him on the last day. For I did not speak on My own, but the Father Himself who sent Me has given Me a commandment as to what to say and what to speak. And I know that His commandment is eternal life; therefore the things I speak, I speak just as the Father has told Me. (John 12:47–50, NASB)

JESUS HAD COMPLETE confidence in His Father. It didn't matter what His Father wanted done, Jesus just did it. Likewise, when His Father wanted something said, Jesus said it. There was nothing complicated about it. Jesus didn't need advisers to counsel Him. He had everything needed to qualify Him to speak. This alone set Him apart from every other person in the world.

Jesus was very clear about how and why He spoke. He said, *"I did not speak on My own."* When He spoke, it was not influenced by how he felt about the activities around Him, or His opinion of others. He simply said the words He heard His Father speak. He didn't leave a single word from God unspoken, nor did He add one word to emphasize it.

Therefore, we can treat every word He spoke as a word from God and have complete confidence that those words will accomplish their purpose. Every word He spoke in the New Testament had a clean, valid purpose.

What about our words? We may not have the same type of father-son relationship Jesus had, but our words are important. The excessive words I use to validate myself will negatively affect my ability to hear God's words and speak them. His words relate to eternal life; mine will always relate to my own temporary life, unless my focus on God is greater than it is on myself.

The more we become aware of the difference between our wasted words and the power of every word God speaks, the more we will be motivated to pray like David: *"Let the words of my mouth, and the meditation of my heart, be acceptable in thy sight, O Lord, my strength, and my redeemer"* (Psalm 19:14, KJV).

CHARACTER VALIDATES OUR WORDS

> And Eli said, "What was it that he told you? Do not hide it from me. May God do so to you and more also if you hide anything from me of all that he told you." So Samuel told him everything and hid nothing from him. And he said, "It is the Lord. Let him do what seems good to him."
>
> And Samuel grew, and the Lord was with him and let none of his words fall to the ground. And all Israel from Dan to Beersheba knew that Samuel was established as a prophet of the Lord. And the Lord appeared again at Shiloh, for the Lord revealed himself to Samuel at Shiloh by the word of the Lord. (1 Samuel 3:17-21, ESV)

SAMUEL HAD A very unusual start in life. His mother was brokenhearted because she couldn't have children. Then, after praying, God blessed her with a son. Somehow she imparted to Samuel her faith and tender-hearted connection to God. Her love for God was proven when she gave her son back to God as soon as he was mature.

Samuel began his work by helping Eli, an old priest whose sons worked in the temple as well. His sons were corrupt, but Eli did nothing about it. His sons wouldn't listen to anything he said because his words had no meaning.

God wasn't pleased with this state of affairs, but this was the atmosphere in which Samuel began to serve. He watched as the priests served themselves while claiming to serve God.

Samuel was young and inexperienced but didn't fall into their way of living: *"But Samuel ministered before the Lord, being a child, girded with a linen ephod"* (1 Samuel 2:18, KJV).

It's a good thing to minister before the Lord, but this involves more than working as a servant. It speaks more to being a worshipper than it does a servant.

Yes, Samuel worshipped the Lord. Maybe it was something he watched his parents do when he was a small boy. Wherever he learned this, he was attracted to the beauty of it. This life shaped his character. He worshipped the Lord while doing physical work for Eli in the temple: *"Now the boy Samuel continued to grow both in stature and in favor with the Lord and also with man"* (1 Samuel 2:26, ESV).

The day finally came when God decided it was time for change. God told Samuel what He was going to do, as well as the reason for it. Samuel told Eli everything, holding nothing back, sharing all that God had told him.

When the day came that Eli and his sons were gone, Samuel remained. God honoured him by not letting one word that Samuel spoke be diminished or disregarded. His character, with God's blessing, established him as a prophet of the Lord.

IT IS YOUR LIFE

> When Moses had finished speaking all these words to all Israel, he said to them, "Take to your heart all the words with which I am warning you today, which you will command your sons to follow carefully, all the words of this Law. For it is not a trivial matter for you; indeed it is your life. And by this word you will prolong your days in the land, which you are about to cross the Jordan to possess." (Deuteronomy 32:45–47, NASB)

MOSES WAS ONE hundred twenty years old when He spoke these words. Israel was ready to go into the land they had been promised, but Moses wouldn't accompany them. Joshua, set to take over the leadership role, was given just enough instructions from God to guarantee success. But the people had to follow His instructions.

> You shall not add to the word which I am commanding you, nor take away from it, so that you may keep the commandments of the Lord your God which I am commanding you. (Deuteronomy 4:2, NASB)

It was extremely important for them to add not one word, or subtract one word, from the instructions God gave them. His words were meant to give them life, but the life would become polluted if they changed anything.

Sadly, that's exactly what they did, bringing extreme hardship on themselves.

God wanted them to command their sons to carefully observe all that He required, but they misunderstood. He meant for them to be influential by living out His words. This would motivate their sons to observe His words. Instead the people established hard rules of conduct, which they themselves couldn't keep, giving their son no godly example to follow.

God meant His words to be about life, but the Israelites saw them as restrictions imposed by a stranger. They didn't recognize God or the power of His word, so His promise to be with them meant nothing. But God still kept His word.

> Then He commissioned Joshua the son of Nun, and said, "Be strong and courageous, for you will bring the sons of Israel into the land which I swore to them, and I will be with you." (Deuteronomy 31:23, NASB)

When God said that He "swore to them," it wasn't just a promise. It is strongly implied that it was spoken to them at least seven times, so they should have been aware of it.

How many times does God have to speak before we listen and believe?

THE POWER OF HIS PROMISE

He is the one who sends his promise throughout the earth. His word travels with great speed. He is the one who sends snow like wool and scatters frost like ashes. He is the one who throws his hailstones like breadcrumbs. Who can withstand his chilling blast? He sends out his word and melts his hailstones. He makes wind blow and water flow. He speaks his word to Jacob, his laws and judicial decisions to Israel. He has done nothing like this for any other nation. The other nations do not know the decisions he has handed down. (Psalm 147:15–20, GW)

Since a king's word has such power, no one can ask him what he is doing. Whoever obeys his commands will avoid trouble. The mind of a wise person will know the right time and the right way to act. (Ecclesiastes 8:4–5, GW)

MOST OF US know that it's not a good idea to make a promise we can't fulfill. It may happen unintentionally, but before long, if done repeatedly, people stop believing anything we say. Trust is easily lost and our words lose meaning. When that happens, our human nature drives us to try adding value by using more and more words. It doesn't work because the problem is in our character, not the number of our words.

When God speaks His word, time and distance have no influence over them. They cannot be limited because they are driven by

His character. Since there is no one like Him, there is no one whose words have the same power.

We are limited by the inferiority of our nature. He is unlimited because He is King of Kings and Lord of Lords. We must become aware of His voice and quickly step in line rather than question Him.

> The heavens declare the glory of God, and the skies announce what his hands have made. Day after day they tell the story; night after night they tell it again. They have no speech or words; they have no voice to be heard. But their message goes out through all the world; their words go everywhere on earth. The sky is like a home for the sun. (Psalm 19:1–4, NCV)

Maybe it's time to slow the pace of our lives, open our eyes, and close our mouths. Let's take the time to look around us and admire His beautiful world. Then we too will obey His words and not bring trouble on ourselves.

WE NEED IT ALL!

> The teachings of the Lord are perfect. They renew the soul. The testimony of the Lord is dependable. It makes gullible people wise. The instructions of the Lord are correct. They make the heart rejoice. The command of the Lord is radiant. It makes the eyes shine. The fear of the Lord is pure. It endures forever. The decisions of the Lord are true. They are completely fair. They are more desirable than gold, even the finest gold. They are sweeter than honey, even the drippings from a honeycomb. As your servant I am warned by them. There is a great reward in following them. (Psalm 19:7–11, GW)

ALL THE DECLARATIONS of God are complete. Nothing is lacking when He gives us His teachings, just like when He declared His words at the beginning of time to create the world. There was no "Oops, I forgot something" as He set everything in order.

God's declarations are energized with purpose. He doesn't need us to clarify or add anything to improve them. Whether I like or dislike what He says, it changes nothing.

Unfortunately, our know-it-all attitudes lead us to analyze and minimize His words as we maximize our own. But there is a way to receive the benefit of what God says. David did it: *"I want to hear what God the Lord says, because he promises peace [safety] to his people, to his godly ones. But they must not go back to their stupidity"* (Psalm 85:8, GW).

David had been in extreme jeopardy many times and had a great appreciation for his times of safety. He was also very aware that his unsafe periods were often the result of stupid things he had done.

When we live according to God's design, we find a sweet beauty that satisfies our deepest hunger. Our lives will be full even if our stomachs are empty and we will know sweet peace even in the midst of raging storms. We will have no need to calm the storm outside if there is only peace inside.

It's better to be on stormy waters with God than on a calm sea without Him.

Day Thirty-Eight
LIVING BY EVERY WORD FROM HIS MOUTH

> And He will judge between many peoples and render decisions for mighty, distant nations. Then they will beat their swords into plowshares, and their spears into pruning hooks; nation will not lift a sword against nation, and never again will they train for war. Instead, each of them will sit under his vine and under his fig tree, with no one to make them afraid, because the mouth of the Lord of armies has spoken. Though all the peoples walk, each in the name of his god, as for us, we will walk in the name of the Lord our God forever and ever. (Micah 4:3–5, NASB)

THE HISTORY OF humanity seems to indicate that big, strong nations often dominate the smaller, weaker ones. When a strong nation wants something from a weaker one, there is an attempt to broker a deal. But if that process fails, a war results—and the stronger nation gets what it wants by using force. Every nation throughout history has needed to be ready for war.

When we live with the continual possibility of war, we stay prepared for it. We use our resources to acquire the tools needed to fight, rather than the tools needed to support healthy, peaceful communities.

In Micah's day, the people needed swords and spears. But this all changed when God stepped in. It was easy for Him; He just began to govern the people and the nations. They were no longer in control. He was. Since they no longer needed weapons to fight and destroy, they worked hard to modify them. Now they had tools for production rather than destruction.

This was the reason for God's intervention. The people's lives no longer resolved around tool preparation and training for war but rather flourishing in a peaceful environment. They could enjoy rest. There was no one to make them afraid. Their peace was guaranteed because the Lord of hosts had spoken.

What would it be like if we lived under God's rule? Would it really mean to use our energy to build up and nourish ourselves and others rather than fight and defend ourselves?

When we have the peace that comes from living under God's government, it will be easy to trust every word coming from the mouth of the Lord.

Day Thirty-Nine
THE PROMISE OF JESUS

But as he considered these things, behold, an angel of the Lord appeared to him in a dream, saying, "Joseph, son of David, do not fear to take Mary as your wife, for that which is conceived in her is from the Holy Spirit. She will bear a son, and you shall call his name Jesus, for he will save his people from their sins."

All this took place to fulfill what the Lord had spoken by the prophet: "Behold, the virgin shall conceive and bear a son, and they shall call his name Immanuel" (which means, God with us). When Joseph woke from sleep, he did as the angel of the Lord commanded him: he took his wife, but knew her not until she had given birth to a son. And he called his name Jesus. (Matthew 1:20–25, ESV)

JOSEPH HAD A difficult problem. He had to figure out what to do about the relationship he had with a young lady, Mary. He loved her and was committed to marriage, but he was shocked to learn that she was expecting a child.

It's hard to imagine the pain and confusion he must have felt. He was a man of good character, wanting to do the right thing.

Only God could bring clarity to a situation like this, so it took an encounter with an angel of the Lord for Joseph to resolve it.

This came as a result of something God had promised more than seven hundred years before: *"Therefore the Lord himself will give you a sign. Behold, the virgin shall conceive and bear a son, and shall call his name Immanuel"* (Isaiah 7:14, ESV).

Since God isn't influenced by time or distance, the promises He made to the prophet Isaiah concerning the coming of the Messiah were as fresh in His mind as they had been the day He spoke them.

While God knew the fulfillment of His promise, though, it was an unexpected interruption in Joseph's life. Thankfully, Joseph did what he was told to do.

Our lives can be very similar, feeling safe in our routines and expecting them to continue until suddenly, by God's design, we find ourselves involved in the execution of something God declared many years ago. God has the ability to get us to focus our attention on the fulfillment of His words rather than the pain of our situations. We are honoured whenever God chooses us to be involved in the working out of His promise.

Life isn't about being free of problems and pain. It's about being reliable and ready to co-labour with God as His promises come to pass.

Day Forty
WORDS WITH COMPASSION

> Now a leper came to Him, imploring Him, kneeling down to Him and saying to Him, "If You are willing, You can make me clean."
> Then Jesus, moved with compassion, stretched out His hand and touched him, and said to him, "I am willing; be cleansed." As soon as He had spoken, immediately the leprosy left him, and he was cleansed. And He strictly warned him and sent him away at once, and said to him, "See that you say nothing to anyone; but go your way, show yourself to the priest, and offer for your cleansing those things which Moses commanded, as a testimony to them." (Mark 1:40–44, NKJV)

I CAN'T IMAGINE what it would have been like to be a leper, living with the required amount of isolation. Their separation from society was meant to protect others from getting the disease, which was good, but it made life very difficult for those who already had it. They weren't known as people *with* the disease; they were known *as* the disease. They were identified as unclean lepers.

It appears only one leper was named in the Bible. Simon was apparently healed, but he continued to be called Simon the leper. There's no clear story of his healing, but he couldn't have had guests in his house if he were still a leper.

Then there's the story of the leper in Mark 1. He came to Jesus, obviously knowing that Jesus could do something about his disease. Questions remained in his mind, though. Would Jesus care enough and be willing to do something to change his unclean condition?

The greatest thrill of this man's life must have come as he watched and listened to Jesus speak with compassion in His voice: *"I am willing; be cleansed."* Then he became aware that he was no longer a leper. It was impossible for him to keep quiet. He told everybody about Jesus!

The words of Jesus, driven by His compassion, can change our lives today just like they did for that leper two thousand years ago. Then we too will want to tell the world about Jesus!

Day Forty-One
BELIEVING

As he traveled through Galilee, he came to Cana, where he had turned the water into wine. There was a government official in nearby Capernaum whose son was very sick. When he heard that Jesus had come from Judea to Galilee, he went and begged Jesus to come to Capernaum to heal his son, who was about to die.

Jesus asked, "Will you never believe in me unless you see miraculous signs and wonders?"

The official pleaded, "Lord, please come now before my little boy dies."

Then Jesus told him, "Go back home. Your son will live!" And the man believed what Jesus said and started home.

While the man was on his way, some of his servants met him with the news that his son was alive and well. (John 4:46–51, NLT)

JESUS WAS ON a journey, one that appears to have begun when He transformed water into wine at a wedding. People noticed Him and thought He was unusual. The things He did couldn't be ignored. He was the kind of person who attracted the broken and needy, but those who were wealthy and self-centred resented Him.

Jesus encountered a man who had a very sick little boy. Obviously, this man had heard enough about Jesus to believe He would care enough to do something. He begged Jesus to come quickly to his house and heal his son before he died.

After the man asked a second time, Jesus simply told him to go home because his son would live.

That's when the healing happened.

Jesus didn't jump at the chance to perform another miracle, because He hadn't come to show what He could do. He came to show the people who He was. This process of showing who He was would require Him to also show what He could do.

This man who wanted his son to live believed Jesus for what He could do and benefited greatly from his belief.

But Jesus wanted to take it a step further—and this man and his entire household took that step. The evidence proved that He cared and it was safe to follow Him. The power of Jesus's words opened the door of faith, and they chose to believe in Him.

Watch for the actions that come from His words to you. They will motivate you to believe in Him.

Day Forty-Two
HEARING OF HIM PROMPTS FAITH IN HIM

But what does it say? "The word is near you, in your mouth and in your heart" (that is, the word of faith that we proclaim); because, if you confess with your mouth that Jesus is Lord and believe in your heart that God raised him from the dead, you will be saved. For with the heart one believes and is justified, and with the mouth one confesses and is saved. For the Scripture says, "Everyone who believes in him will not be put to shame." For there is no distinction between Jew and Greek; for the same Lord is Lord of all, bestowing his riches on all who call on him. For "everyone who calls on the name of the Lord will be saved."

How then will they call on him in whom they have not believed? And how are they to believe in him of whom they have never heard? And how are they to hear without someone preaching? And how are they to preach unless they are sent? As it is written, "How beautiful are the feet of those who preach the good news!" (Romans 10:8–15, ESV)

THE ACTIONS OF our lives don't occur in isolation. It would probably be safe to say that most of the things we do aren't independent actions at all but reactions to what's already happening. God programmed our bodies to respond to the life around us. However, because of His love for us, He gave us a choice. We aren't programmed robots; our actions and reactions are all the result of choices.

In His wisdom, God set in motion a series of events to stimulate us to call on Him for salvation. It all started with someone being sent to preach, and that preaching made it possible for us to hear about Him. Once the truth about Him entered our hearts, it was easy to believe in Him. The result of believing in Him stimulated us to choose to call on Him to intervene in our lives and save us.

Psalm 119:130 tells us, *"The entrance of Your words gives light; it gives understanding to the simple"* (Psalm 119:130, NKJV). The entrance of His words into our lives can come in quiet, simple ways. It can also be extremely dramatic. Some people forsook all they had and began to follow Jesus after hearing Him say just two words: "Follow me." With others, it was different.

The apostle Paul got knocked off his horse. Blinded by a light, he was so overpowered that all he could ask was "Who are you and what do you want me to do?"

In the case of Paul and Jesus's disciples, they believed, obeyed, and followed.

This is the awesome influence of the power of God's words entering our hearts, stimulating us to believe in Him so securely that we leave everything else to serve Him. Nothing else can satisfy the emptiness we had in our hearts before we knew Him.

The joy of salvation consistently drives all our actions and reactions. This is the mark of salvation.

Day Forty-Three
DRIVEN BY HUNGER

Break open your words, let the light shine out, let ordinary people see the meaning. Mouth open and panting, I wanted your commands more than anything. Turn my way, look kindly on me, as you always do to those who personally love you. Steady my steps with your Word of promise so nothing malign gets the better of me. Rescue me from the grip of bad men and women so I can live life your way. Smile on me, your servant; teach me the right way to live. I cry rivers of tears because nobody's living by your book! (Psalm 119:130–136, MSG)

HUNGER IS A powerful motivator. When a person is really hungry, they'll eat almost anything that's available. The way it looks and tastes matters less and less as the hunger intensifies. The only factor that matters becomes this question: "Will it satisfy my hunger?"

What is it that makes a person feel hungry? The simplest explanation is that the sensation arrives from one's stomach muscles contracting more than normal when it empties. The stomach needs to be filled to prevent it from shrinking. This is actually a safety factor, one that God built into us when we were created. We must continually eat if we want to stay alive and keep moving.

This is true both for our natural lives as well as our spiritual lives.

When the disciples asked Jesus to teach them to pray, He showed them the required pattern. Part of that prayer contained a seven-word sentence that makes a difference between life and death: *"Give us this day our daily bread"* (Matthew 6:11, KJV).

When Jesus used the word "daily," He wasn't trying to teach the disciples to ask for bread every twenty-four hours. It was more important than that. He was teaching them to ask for the bread that was necessary. This isn't the bread that fills the stomach; it's the bread that fills the soul.

What would our world be like if we were all so hungry for such real bread that we jumped at the chance to get hold of it? Maybe I don't jump to eat this bread because I'm deriving satisfaction from things apart from heaven.

Dear God, let us experience such intense hunger for the true bread of life that we are driven to jump at every opportunity to partake of it. Amen.

Day Forty-Four
THE PLACE OF GOD'S ADVICE

> When my heart was filled with bitterness and my mind was seized with envy, I was stupid, and I did not understand. I was like a dumb animal in your presence. Yet, I am always with you. You hold on to my right hand. With your advice you guide me, and in the end you will take me to glory. As long as I have you, I don't need anyone else in heaven or on earth. My body and mind may waste away, but God remains the foundation of my life and my inheritance forever. (Psalm 73:21–26, GW)

IT'S A GREAT feeling when someone gives us advice when we're working through unfamiliar situations, especially when we know that the result of our decision will have a large, long-lasting effect on our lives. Sometimes we can't find someone who's been through the same thing we're experiencing, so we don't trust people's advice. But when someone understands what we're going through, because they've experienced it, we feel secure taking their advice.

Somehow David felt secure enough to take God's advice. Maybe it was the sensation of God holding his right hand, or the fact that he'd taken God's advice before and it proved perfect. He never regretted taking His advice.

One thing was sure: God's words of advice to David never turned out to offer a temporary solution. The advice gave him enough security to declare there would be glory, not failure, at the end of one's journey. It wasn't that he never did anything dumb; it was that God was the only foundation in his life.

David had great admiration for God. He obviously felt like a dumb animal when he came into the presence of God and grew aware of their differences. That all changed when he discovered the perfect advice from God:

> You are my hiding place. You protect me from trouble. You surround me with joyous songs of salvation. Selah
>
> The Lord says, "I will instruct you. I will teach you the way that you should go. I will advise you as my eyes watch over you. Don't be stubborn like a horse or mule. They need a bit and bridle in their mouth to restrain them, or they will not come near you." (Psalm 32:7–9, GW)

The promise given to David has been given to us as well, but it's only effective when we live in a relationship with Him, knowing the joyous salvation that comes from His protection in times of trouble.

After all these promises, God cautioned David not to be like a horse or mule, needing a bridle in his mouth to force him to go where he was needed. Such animals lacked so much awareness of reality that it was impossible for them to think new thoughts except for the ones they stubbornly held onto.

When we become aware that God is our hiding place, we quickly discover His words of advice—and they keep us securely anchored to Him.

Day Forty-Five
"I AM JESUS"

Your Majesty, at noon, while I was traveling, I saw a light that was brighter than the sun. The light came from the sky and shined around me and those who were with me. All of us fell to the ground, and I heard a voice asking me in Hebrew, "Saul, Saul! Why are you persecuting me? It's hard for a mortal like you to resist God."

I asked, "Who are you, sir?"

The Lord answered, "I am Jesus, the one you're persecuting. Stand up! I have appeared to you for a reason. I'm appointing you to be a servant and witness of what you have seen and of what I will show you. I will rescue you from the Jewish people and from the non-Jewish people to whom I am sending you. You will open their eyes and turn them from darkness to light and from Satan's control to God's. Then they will receive forgiveness for their sins and a share among God's people who are made holy by believing in me." (Acts 26:13–18, GW)

DURING HIS ENCOUNTER with Jesus, Saul found himself lying on the ground, aware of the authority in the voice speaking to him. The words he heard weren't just empty chatter; they were driven by the authority of the God of the universe. He knew his only option was to take notice and respond properly.

He didn't respond out of arrogance. He didn't say, "Who do you think you are? Do you know who I am?" Instead he asked, *"Who are you, sir?"* He knew he was speaking to someone of greater authority than himself, so he listened carefully.

The answer he received must have stunned him. Saul was a great scholar and diligently practiced all the rules imposed by the religious leaders. He believed in the writings of the prophets and the promises of the coming Messiah. But when the evidence of the Messiah was right in front of him, he tried to destroy it rather than believe it.

Then he heard those decisive words: *"I am Jesus..."* No shouting, no yelling, no drama. Just "I am Jesus." Those words changed the focus of Saul's life.

The next question he asked is fitting for everyone who encounters Jesus: *"Lord, what do You want me to do?"* (Acts 9:6, NKJV) He knew he was no longer a scholar, but a servant, so he didn't ask about what he should believe, but rather what he should do.

Jesus gave us a perfect example of this, since He came to do the works of His Father.

When we get to know Him by seeing Him in action, doing His Father's work, our hunger to serve Him will drive us to ask, "Lord, what do you want me to do?"

Day Forty-Six
THE REASON HIS WORDS HAVE POWER

In your lives you must think and act like Christ Jesus. Christ himself was like God in everything. But he did not think that being equal with God was something to be used for his own benefit. But he gave up his place with God and made himself nothing. He was born as a man and became like a servant. And when he was living as a man, he humbled himself and was fully obedient to God, even when that caused his death—death on a cross. So God raised him to the highest place. God made his name greater than every other name so that every knee will bow to the name of Jesus—everyone in heaven, on earth, and under the earth. And everyone will confess that Jesus Christ is Lord and bring glory to God the Father.

My dear friends, you have always obeyed God when I was with you. It is even more important that you obey now while I am away from you. Keep on working to complete your salvation with fear and trembling… (Philippians 2:5–13, NCV)

EVERYONE LISTENED WHEN Jesus spoke. Some were very attracted to Him and His words, while others got angry and criticized everything He said. These reactions don't come to people who jabber away, pretending to know everything. Those who speak empty words don't get much of a reaction except to be mostly ignored.

Jesus is a perfect example of one whose words were powerful. He came into the world to do the most important job of all time:

to redeem the whole world. I can't imagine how the weight of that responsibility felt. When a person has a very big job, they usually grasp at all the authority and resources available to make the job a bit easier. Jesus did the opposite. He had it all but let everything go, using none of His authority for His benefit.

He knew exactly what he had, and He knew what to do with it. He said, *"The Father loves the Son and has given him power over everything"* (John 3:35, NCV). While He had all this power and authority, He never once used it to exult Himself. Why? Because He knew that the work would extend way beyond His thirty-three years on the earth. His time here was limited, but His powerful effect was eternal.

Jesus came to the earth as a human, then lowered Himself to live as a servant. You can always trust the words of those who choose to lower themselves for the benefit of others. Their words will always lift up and edify others, and never promote themselves.

While Jesus was mocked and belittled, He always honoured His Father. One day His name will be declared throughout the earth and every knee will bow. Every word He ever spoke will be honoured.

WE SPEAK OF JESUS RATHER THAN EXPECTED EVENTS

During the forty days after he suffered and died, he appeared to the apostles from time to time, and he proved to them in many ways that he was actually alive. And he talked to them about the Kingdom of God.

Once when he was eating with them, he commanded them, "Do not leave Jerusalem until the Father sends you the gift he promised, as I told you before. John baptized with water, but in just a few days you will be baptized with the Holy Spirit."

So when the apostles were with Jesus, they kept asking him, "Lord, has the time come for you to free Israel and restore our kingdom?"

He replied, "The Father alone has the authority to set those dates and times, and they are not for you to know. But you will receive power when the Holy Spirit comes upon you. And you will be my witnesses, telling people about me everywhere—in Jerusalem, throughout Judea, in Samaria, and to the ends of the earth."

After saying this, he was taken up into a cloud while they were watching, and they could no longer see him. As they strained to see him rising into heaven, two white-robed men suddenly stood among them. "Men of Galilee," they said, "why are you standing here staring into heaven? Jesus has been taken from you into heaven, but someday he will return from heaven in the same way you saw him go!" (Acts 1:3–11, NLT)

THE DISCIPLES HAD a problem, probably the same one their forefathers had. They wondered when God's promises would be fulfilled. They were aware of the promise of personal freedom, and national independence, but they didn't know why they were here or what they were supposed to do.

The only way Jesus could get them to stop trying to figure out the timing of all God had promised was basically to tell them, "It's none of your business. God knows and that's good enough." At the same time, He wanted them to know what their priority should be—and it wasn't about getting more information regarding God's action or the timing of His promises. It was about knowing how, when, and where to tell people about Jesus, and showing how He lived His life. It was a job they didn't have the ability to finish, so they'd need to wait until they were energized with the Breath of God, the Holy Spirit.

The tragedy in the Christian world today is that we so easily start thinking like the disciples. We claim many promises and hold so many expectations simply because of who we claim to be. The result of that attitude is a huge distraction. Before long, all our words and actions are about ourselves. There's no testimony of Jesus; it's all about us.

This all changes when we're close to Him and listen to His words. As He said, *"And you will be my witnesses, telling people about me everywhere."* What an honour! There is only one saviour, and His name is Jesus!

Day Forty-Eight
LOVING HIM MOTIVATES OBEDIENCE TO HIS WORDS

If you love me, obey my commandments… Those who accept my commandments and obey them are the ones who love me. And because they love me, my Father will love them. And I will love them and reveal myself to each of them…

All who love me will do what I say. My Father will love them, and we will come and make our home with each of them. Anyone who doesn't love me will not obey me. And remember, my words are not my own. What I am telling you is from the Father who sent me. I am telling you these things now while I am still with you. But when the Father sends the Advocate as my representative—that is, the Holy Spirit—he will teach you everything and will remind you of everything I have told you. (John 14:15, 21, 23–26, NLT)

But those who obey God's word truly show how completely they love him. That is how we know we are living in him. Those who say they live in God should live their lives as Jesus did. (1 John 2:5–6, NLT)

THERE IS A clear connection between who we love and whose instructions we follow. We'll never voluntarily follow the instructions of someone we disregard. When we have minimal esteem for a person, their words have little meaning for us.

However, when we have a relationship with someone we highly regard, their words have a lot of meaning. It's very easy to follow their directives.

Jesus often advised us to keep His commandments if we loved Him. It could also be said this way: "When you love me, you will keep my commandments." When we do what He wants us to do, what will our motivation be?

When I see His desires as a commandment, there will be no love attached to my actions. I'll do what He wants because I'm afraid of punishment. When love is absent, fear is the driving force behind obedience. But when love is present, it's impossible for fear to motivate us.

> Where God's love is, there is no fear, because God's perfect love drives out fear. It is punishment that makes a person fear, so love is not made perfect in the person who fears. (1 John 4:18, NCV)

If I have no relationship with Jesus, I won't have His love in my life. The only reason we can love Him is because we know He loved us first (1 John 4:19).

This love gives me a great desire to do what He wants. I don't see His words as commandments that must be obeyed to avoid punishment; I see them as windows into His heart, from which I easily see His desires for me.

Day Forty-Nine
LETTING HIS WORD BE DONE

> And Mary said, "Behold, the Lord's bond-servant; may it be done to me according to your word." And the angel departed from her.
> Now at this time Mary set out and went in a hurry to the hill country, to a city of Judah, and she entered the house of Zechariah and greeted Elizabeth. When Elizabeth heard Mary's greeting, the baby leaped in her womb, and Elizabeth was filled with the Holy Spirit. And she cried out with a loud voice and said, "Blessed are you among women, and blessed is the fruit of your womb! And how has it happened to me that the mother of my Lord would come to me? For behold, when the sound of your greeting reached my ears, the baby leaped in my womb for joy. And blessed is she who believed that there would be a fulfillment of what had been spoken to her by the Lord." (Luke 1:38–45, NASB)

GOD HAD HIS eye on Mary, but she had no idea of the plan being implemented. She had lived her life honourably and looked forward to being married to Joseph.

She probably appeared similar to all the other young ladies in Nazareth, having no sense of entitlement or expectation of the special word that was about to be given to her. She was shocked when the angel appeared. She heard the words but kept wondering, *What's going on?*

And coming in, he said to her, "Greetings, favored one! The Lord is with you." But she was very perplexed at this statement, and was pondering what kind of greeting this was. (Luke 1:28–29, NASB)

God often gets the attention of His chosen servants in a unique way. But no matter how God gets their attention, they are shocked when they discover God's been watching them and formulating plans for their lives. They don't see themselves as special. They have no expectation of praise or special recognition. Instead they are greatly surprised when God shows His plan and their involvement in it.

Mary responded with a perfect heart, identifying herself as a slave of the Lord, with no plans or expectations of her own. She had questions about how all this was going to work, though, and the angel provided specific details. There must have been other things she wondered about, but her final response was simple: *"may it be done to me according to your word."*

The word of the Lord can come to us in many different ways. How it comes isn't really important. The important part is that we respond with openness and commit our lives to be ready for Him to do whatever fits His plans.

God isn't looking for entitled, highly qualified and recognized people. He's looking for quiet, humble, unrecognized people living in ordinary places; their hearts cause them to respond like Mary. They won't question the outcome of His words but rather respond in confidence that every word will be perfectly accomplished.

THE RESULTS OF OBEYING HIS WORD

And when he had finished speaking, he said to Simon, "Put out into the deep and let down your nets for a catch."

And Simon answered, "Master, we toiled all night and took nothing! But at your word I will let down the nets."

And when they had done this, they enclosed a large number of fish, and their nets were breaking. They signaled to their partners in the other boat to come and help them. And they came and filled both the boats, so that they began to sink.

But when Simon Peter saw it, he fell down at Jesus' knees, saying, "Depart from me, for I am a sinful man, O Lord." For he and all who were with him were astonished at the catch of fish that they had taken, and so also were James and John, sons of Zebedee, who were partners with Simon.

And Jesus said to Simon, "Do not be afraid; from now on you will be catching men."

And when they had brought their boats to land, they left everything and followed him. (Luke 5:4–11, ESV)

THERE IS AN explosive dynamic in these words of Jesus, and it was demonstrated every time he gave someone detailed instructions about what to do. Every time people did what He said, there was an immediate result. Something always happened.

We can probably all identify with Peter after he worked all night but didn't catch any fish. That tired, unfulfilled feeling takes away one's desire to keep working. It may seem like all we need is a good break, to regain our energy. The last thing we need is for someone to tell us to try again. Repeated failure convinces us that only more failure is ahead. So we stop trying, and getting us to try again will require more than logical arguments.

Jesus proved that He was more than enough to prevent failure. His words of instruction to Peter didn't indicate that he *might* catch fish, but that he *would* catch fish. Peter then believed and acted on His words! He did this despite the previous night's failure.

They not only caught some fish; they caught twice as many fish as their boat could handle.

Before this event, Peter's life had been about fishing and interacting with his friends, one of whom was Jesus. Yes, Jesus was just a friend. He was a lot like all the other friends he enjoyed being around.

When Peter obeyed the words of Jesus, not only did his boat get full, but his heart filled as well. He saw Jesus for who He was. He also saw himself for who he was, and it must have made him afraid.

Again, the powerful words of Jesus had their effect. It wasn't about fish, or fear. It was about following. The disciples left behind the fish and their fathers in order to follow Jesus. The rest of the story is now history.

When you hear His word to you, what will your story be like?

Day Fifty-One
JESUS PRAYED FOR US

But now I am coming to You; and these things I speak in the world so that they may have My joy made full in themselves. I have given them Your word; and the world has hated them because they are not of the world, just as I am not of the world. I am not asking You to take them out of the world, but to keep them away from the evil one. They are not of the world, just as I am not of the world. Sanctify them in the truth; Your word is truth. Just as You sent Me into the world, I also sent them into the world. (John 17:13–18, NASB)

JESUS PRAYED TO His Father, expressing His desire for the ones who followed Him. It's clear that Jesus had a definite reason for telling what He did. His goal wasn't to attract followers by impressing them with His speaking skills or knowledge. His goal wasn't about getting something from His followers, but about *giving* them something.

He spoke truth everywhere so everyone could be filled with the same joy that filled Him. This wasn't the kind of temporary happiness one gets when all life is going well; it was the calm delight of being anchored to God, reaching out to Him during every difficult experience.

Jesus treasured this joy so highly that He wanted all His followers to have it. This is the joy that carried Him while He was on the cross. He showed us how joy could motivate us during our greatest troubles:

> Let us look only to Jesus, the One who began our faith and who makes it perfect. He suffered death on

the cross. But he accepted the shame as if it were nothing because of the joy that God put before him. And now he is sitting at the right side of God's throne. Think about Jesus' example. He held on while wicked people were doing evil things to him. So do not get tired and stop trying. (Hebrews 12:2–3, NCV)

The words Jesus spoke carried more than a message. They carried His spirit, which stimulates action in our lives. Somehow all the shame that was put on Him, and all the false accusations of those who hated Him, could not distract Him from the strong pull of the joy He saw ahead. He knew the calm of His Father's presence even while going through the worst thing any person could endure.

Jesus wants us to have the same joy! Take His words to heart and receive what He wants to give.

THE LORD'S GLORY IN WORDS AND ACTIONS

I give you thanks, O Lord, with my whole heart; before the God's I sing your praise; I bow down toward your holy temple and give thanks to your name for your steadfast love and your faithfulness, for you have exalted above all things your name and your word. On the day I called, you answered me; my strength of soul you increased.

All the kings of the earth shall give you thanks, O Lord, for they have heard the words of your mouth, and they shall sing of the ways of the Lord, for great is the glory of the Lord. For though the Lord is high, he regards the lowly, but the haughty he knows from afar.

Though I walk in the midst of trouble, you preserve my life; you stretch out your hand against the wrath of my enemies, and your right hand delivers me. The Lord will fulfill his purpose for me; your steadfast love, O Lord, endures forever. Do not forsake the work of your hands. (Psalm 138:1–8, ESV)

THE CHARACTER OF God is so uniquely perfect that it's hard for us to understand Him. But when we begin to discover His perfection, we are overcome with thanksgiving. The continuous love and faithfulness He gives us is the anchor that brings stability when it looks like we're about to lose everything.

God's character is so superior that even those who reign as kings in this world are driven to greatly appreciate Him. Sometimes people with authority can appreciate those with greater authority more quickly than those who have never had it.

Thankfully, God doesn't just let His beauty be seen by kings who have the power to rule over us. He is also aware of the humble ones, those who have nothing and are more likely to be put down than lifted up.

God reveals Himself in two ways—through His name and His word. He perfectly aligns what He does and what He says. In fact, His actions and words are so intertwined that they can't be separated. His words describe Him and His actions reveal Him—and when we encounter Him, we discover that He is everything He says.

When we call on Him, we are bestowed the greatest possible honour, for He hears our cry and responds. Then we will know the changing power of Him and His words.

THE BEAUTIFUL WORDS OF JESUS

> A woman in the crowd had suffered for twelve years with constant bleeding, and she could find no cure. Coming up behind Jesus, she touched the fringe of his robe. Immediately, the bleeding stopped.
>
> "Who touched me?" Jesus asked.
>
> Everyone denied it, and Peter said, "Master, this whole crowd is pressing up against you."
>
> But Jesus said, "Someone deliberately touched me, for I felt healing power go out from me." When the woman realized that she could not stay hidden, she began to tremble and fell to her knees in front of him. The whole crowd heard her explain why she had touched him and that she had been immediately healed.
>
> "Daughter," he said to her, "your faith has made you well. Go in peace." (Luke 8:43–48, NLT)

THE EVENTS OF this passage probably represent just another busy day for Jesus, who was often surrounded by large crowds as He walked. I can only imagine the chaos. People were talking and laughing. Some moved in painful silence, no doubt wondering what to do, for they had come with a specific purpose. Still others came to Him out of curiosity. One thing was certain: if you stayed in the crowd long enough, you would probably see something amazing.

One woman in the crowd was different than the others. She had a huge problem that troubled her every day. She'd spent all her money trying to get help, but nothing had worked. Her bleeding had left her physically weak and caused her to be ceremonially unclean, preventing her from participating in temple activities. She was broken and bleeding, defiled and dejected.

At the same time, she had a spark of hope in her heart.

This woman didn't want attention; she only wanted healing. She had heard about Jesus and knew that He could heal her if she could only touch the very bottom of His garment. That would be enough.

A similar healing had happened before when He had been in Gennesaret: *"They begged him to let the sick touch at least the fringe of his robe, and all who touched him were healed"* (Matthew 14:36, NLT).

When she touched Jesus, He knew this was no accidental bump but a deliberate touch done in faith. She had an expectation and she wasn't disappointed. She was instantly healed!

Then Jesus spoke the most beautiful words she had ever heard: *"Daughter, your faith has made you well. Go in peace."*

BELIEVING HIS WORDS MOTIVATES OUR ACTIONS

Now when Mary came to where Jesus was and saw him, she fell at his feet, saying to him, "Lord, if you had been here, my brother would not have died."

When Jesus saw her weeping, and the Jews who had come with her also weeping, he was deeply moved in his spirit and greatly troubled. And he said, "Where have you laid him?"

They said to him, "Lord, come and see."

Jesus wept.

So the Jews said, "See how he loved him!" But some of them said, "Could not he who opened the eyes of the blind man also have kept this man from dying?"

Then Jesus, deeply moved again, came to the tomb. It was a cave, and a stone lay against it.

Jesus said, "Take away the stone."

Martha, the sister of the dead man, said to him, "Lord, by this time there will be an odor, for he has been dead four days."

Jesus said to her, "Did I not tell you that if you believed you would see the glory of God?"

So they took away the stone. And Jesus lifted up his eyes and said, "Father, I thank you that you have heard me. I knew that you always hear me, but I said this on account of the people standing around, that they may believe that you sent me."

When he had said these things, he cried out with a loud voice, "Lazarus, come out." The man who had died came out, his hands and feet bound with linen strips, and his face wrapped with a cloth. Jesus said to them, "Unbind him, and let him go." (John 11:32–44, ESV)

IT CAN BE hard to understand why God allows painful things to happen to us. We're often a lot like Mary in this passage. She had enough faith to believe that her brother Lazarus could have been healed if only Jesus had been physically present at the time of his death. Her questions sound a lot like ours: "Why weren't you here? Where were you?"

God knew how to get Lazarus out of the grave, even though his family saw no way. It was hard for them to consider the possibility of a miracle. He'd been dead so long that he stunk.

But as they communicated with Jesus, and did what He said, they were treated to a spectacular display of God's glory.

Jesus could have told everyone to stand back while he rolled away the stone, but He didn't. He could have unwrapped the cloth from Lazarus's hands, feet, and face. But He didn't. He told *them* to do it.

The only thing He did was the thing they couldn't: speak words that would bring him out of the grave. Those words awoke a dead man and called him out of the grave. Whether we are dead or alive, in the grave or outside it, the words of Jesus will always inspire us to take action.

Day Fifty-Five
JESUS'S WORDS BRING REALITY

> While Jesus was speaking, a crowd came up, and Judas, one of the twelve apostles, was leading them. He came close to Jesus so he could kiss him. But Jesus said to him, "Judas, are you using the kiss to give the Son of Man to his enemies?"
>
> When those who were standing around him saw what was happening, they said, "Lord, should we strike them with our swords?" And one of them struck the servant of the high priest and cut off his right ear.
>
> Jesus said, "Stop! No more of this." Then he touched the servant's ear and healed him. (Luke 22:47–51, NCV)

THIS ENCOUNTER BETWEEN Jesus and Judas came after Jesus and His disciples had spent a night upon a mountain. Jesus knew the suffering that was ahead, so His prayer was intense. Ultimately, He committed Himself, and everything that was to happen, into His Father's hands.

God's plan began to unfold very quickly. A good-sized crowd approached Jesus, with Judas leading them. When Judas walked right up to Jesus, it was obvious that he intended to do something significant.

The kiss was a terrible betrayal. Judas had to have known that those watching it would assume the men shared an intimate bond. The kiss could be used to show mutual affection, or it could be used to reaffirm a covenant.

This time, it was used as a signal to identify the one these soldiers had come to kill.

Jesus asked a very penetrating question: *"Judas, are you using the kiss to give the Son of Man to his enemies?"* This was the opportunity for Judas to consider the words of Jesus and correct what he was about to do.

But he didn't.

Eventually, Judas came to realize the awfulness of his actions. His betrayal of Jesus, while trying to make himself look good, produced in him a torment he couldn't live with.

Jesus has the ability to expose the wrong attitudes of a person's heart even while their outside activities look noble. However, we decide what to do when His words expose our hearts.

May the actions of my lips, whether speaking or kissing, be a true testimony of my heart.

WHEN JESUS ASKS A QUESTION

Now Jesus called His disciples to Him and said, "I feel compassion for the people, because they have remained with Me now for three days and have nothing to eat; and I do not want to send them away hungry, for they might faint on the way."

The disciples said to Him, "Where would we get so many loaves in this desolate place to satisfy such a large crowd?"

And Jesus said to them, "How many loaves do you have?"

And they said, "Seven, and a few small fish."

And He directed the people to sit down on the ground; and He took the seven loaves and the fish; and after giving thanks, He broke them and started giving them to the disciples, and the disciples gave them to the crowds. And they all ate and were satisfied, and they picked up what was left over of the broken pieces, seven large baskets full. And those who ate were four thousand men, besides women and children.

And sending away the crowds, Jesus got into the boat and came to the region of Magadan. (Matthew 15:32–39, NASB)

AT TIMES, THOUSANDS of people gathered to watch Jesus and listen to Him teach. Most of them probably brought some food, not knowing how long they would stay. But one day, when it came time to eat and the people prepared to return home, Jesus noticed that there was very little food.

The disciples' response would have seemed to be quite normal. They knew they didn't have enough food, so they tried to get more. But they quickly concluded that it wouldn't be possible. There were too many people and their distance from the nearest town too great.

Jesus had a different thought process. He didn't focus on what they didn't have or how far away it was. None of that mattered to Him. He asked them one question: *"How many loaves do you have?"* The disciples were limited by what they didn't have and couldn't get. Their limited perception made it impossible to be thankful and share what they themselves possessed.

Listen for the question Jesus would ask you. What do you have to give?

WHAT DO YOU WANT ME TO DO FOR YOU?

Now they came to Jericho. As He went out of Jericho with His disciples and a great multitude, blind Bartimaeus, the son of Timaeus, sat by the road begging. And when he heard that it was Jesus of Nazareth, he began to cry out and say, "Jesus, Son of David, have mercy on me!"

Then many warned him to be quiet; but he cried out all the more, "Son of David, have mercy on me!"

So Jesus stood still and commanded him to be called.

Then they called the blind man, saying to him, "Be of good cheer. Rise, He is calling you."

And throwing aside his garment, he rose and came to Jesus.

So Jesus answered and said to him, "What do you want Me to do for you?"

The blind man said to Him, "Rabboni, that I may receive my sight."

Then Jesus said to him, "Go your way; your faith has made you well." And immediately he received his sight and followed Jesus on the road. (Mark 10:46–52, NKJV)

DARTIMAEUS WAS DOING what he had to do to survive. He was blind and everyone knew it. When people walked by, they noticed that he couldn't see. It appears that no one saw the desperate desire in his heart to see.

Everything changed in a moment.

As soon as Bartimaeus heard that Jesus was in the crowd, he called to Him with a loud, desperate cry, begging for mercy—the kind of mercy that could change his world. His cry made some people uncomfortable. They didn't know what it was to hurt so much, to live a life with so much wrong that only a merciful encounter with Jesus could correct it. These comfortable ones didn't like being uncomfortable. They didn't appreciate the distracting noise of this man's loud cry—until they saw that Jesus paid attention.

They were such hypocrites. Suddenly, they pretended to care.

Bartimaeus's cry got him into the presence of Jesus. Then Jesus spoke nine words to him: *"What do you want Me to do for you?"* This question unlocked the door of faith and Bartimaeus received his sight.

Set aside religious propriety and call out to Jesus with your whole heart. He will be there for you, just like He was for Bartimaeus. The words of Jesus are for you too. What do *you* want Me to do for *you*?"

Day Fifty-Eight
HIS WORDS BROUGHT NO CONDEMNATION

As he was speaking, the teachers of religious law and the Pharisees brought a woman who had been caught in the act of adultery. They put her in front of the crowd.

"Teacher," they said to Jesus, "this woman was caught in the act of adultery. The law of Moses says to stone her. What do you say?"

They were trying to trap him into saying something they could use against him, but Jesus stooped down and wrote in the dust with his finger. They kept demanding an answer, so he stood up again and said, "All right, but let the one who has never sinned throw the first stone!" Then he stooped down again and wrote in the dust.

When the accusers heard this, they slipped away one by one, beginning with the oldest, until only Jesus was left in the middle of the crowd with the woman. Then Jesus stood up again and said to the woman, "Where are your accusers? Didn't even one of them condemn you?"

"No, Lord," she said.

And Jesus said, "Neither do I. Go and sin no more. (John 8:3–11, NLT)

A WOMAN WAS facing death by stoning. She'd been caught breaking a legitimate law that came with a punishment. There would be no trial, since the ones who accused her had already determined that she should be stoned.

These accusers are noted as *"teachers of religious law and the Pharisees."* They were very active in seeking out those who broke their laws, condemning them with the harshest punishments possible, even death by stoning. They looked for ways to condemn anyone who didn't promote their system of right and wrong.

Jesus was one of their targets as well, and they used their condemnation of this guilty woman to find fault with Him.

Jesus's response was brilliant. With His finger, He wrote something in the dust. He didn't point to them and accuse them of wrong deeds. This appears to be the only time in the Bible that Jesus wrote something, and we can only speculate about what He wrote. Whatever it was, they paid no attention to it.

When they kept demanding a verbal reply, He stood up and gave them an answer. His words ended their condemnation and they walked away. Again, He bent down and wrote with His finger in the dust.

On this day, a guilty woman heard the most powerful words anyone can hear: *"Didn't even one of them condemn you? Neither do I."*

Day Fifty-Nine
"WHO DO YOU SAY I AM?"

When Jesus came to the area of Caesarea Philippi, he asked his followers, "Who do people say the Son of Man is?"

They answered, "Some say you are John the Baptist. Others say you are Elijah, and still others say you are Jeremiah or one of the prophets."

Then Jesus asked them, "And who do you say I am?"

Simon Peter answered, "You are the Christ, the Son of the living God."

Jesus answered, "You are blessed, Simon son of Jonah, because no person taught you that. My Father in heaven showed you who I am. (Matthew 16:13–17, NCV)

WHEN JESUS ASKED a question, it wasn't because He lacked information. Rather, He wanted to get His disciples to stop and think about who He was. It was also important for them not to identify Him by comparing Him with others. Even though they had all watched Him do the same things, they obviously didn't all agree on who He was. They compared Him to prophets of old who had performed similar miracles.

But Jesus wasn't like anyone else. As the Son of God, He brought a new standard of living. The disciples saw His life and everything He did, but they were also becoming aware of who He was. Jesus wanted them to get to know Him for who He was, not just for what He did.

The religious leaders of the day were aware of all the writings of the prophets detailing the coming Messiah. They studied these scriptures often and formed rigid opinions. They were sure they would recognize Him when He came.

But when He came, they didn't know it was Him.

The disciples, too, were aware of these same prophetic foretellings, but they had a heart-to-heart connection with Jesus. Because of this relationship, God was able to open their eyes and show them that Jesus was the Messiah.

When Jesus asked them to identify who He was, they became conscious that He was the Christ, the one appointed and anointed to be the Messiah, the Son of God. Peter got it right and Jesus was clear that the answer didn't come from him, but from God.

If Jesus were to ask you the same question—*"And who do you say I am?"*—would your answer come from the information you'd gathered or from your experience of a living relationship with Him?

ARE YOU DETERMINED TO GET WELL?

Now in Jerusalem, by the Sheep Gate, there is a pool which in Hebrew is called Bethesda, having five porticoes. In these porticoes lay a multitude of those who were sick, blind, limping, or paralyzed.

Now a man was there who had been ill for thirty-eight years. Jesus, upon seeing this man lying there and knowing that he had already been in that condition for a long time, said to him, "Do you want to get well?"

The sick man answered Him, "Sir, I have no man to put me into the pool when the water is stirred up, but while I am coming, another steps down before me."

Jesus said to him, "Get up, pick up your pallet and walk."

Immediately the man became well, and picked up his pallet and began to walk.

Now it was a Sabbath on that day. So the Jews were saying to the man who was cured, "It is a Sabbath, and it is not permissible for you to carry your pallet." (John 5:2–10, NASB)

THIS PASSAGE REVEALS a man who had been crippled for thirty-eight years, but he never gave up. He stayed by this pool, surrounded by other cripples, waiting and hoping for a chance to be the first in the pool when the water was stirred.

So far he had never made it, because others always got to the water ahead of him.

There must have been some kind of hope in his heart to keep him there, lying on his little bed, believing that some day he would be healed. He still had hope, even after trying and failing for thirty-eight years. I can only imagine how sad and tired he must have looked. He could have easily been the saddest one there.

When Jesus came to the pool, He noticed this man and asked him a question. The man's answer strongly indicated that he hadn't just been lying there; every time the water was stirred, his hopeful expectation drove him to do everything he could to reach the water.

But he needed help.

Jesus spoke words that gave this man a whole new life: *"Get up..."* The crippled man suddenly had no problem putting in the effort. He had been trying for thirty-eight years, yes, but now everything had changed; he was empowered by the words of Jesus.

He simply got up, picked up his bed, and walked away from his former life as a cripple. We can do the same when we hear the words of Jesus.

WHOEVER HUMBLES HIMSELF IS THE GREATEST

At that time the disciples came to Jesus and said, "Who then is greatest in the kingdom of heaven?"

And He called a child to Himself and set him among them, and said, "Truly I say to you, unless you change and become like children, you will not enter the kingdom of heaven. So whoever will humble himself like this child, he is the greatest in the kingdom of heaven. And whoever receives one such child in My name, receives Me; but whoever causes one of these little ones who believe in Me to sin, it is better for him that a heavy millstone be hung around his neck, and that he be drowned in the depths of the sea. (Matthew 18:1–6, NASB)

SINCE THE BEGINNING of time, we've all felt the urge in our hearts to be in charge. Competition between people always comes down to finding out who is the greatest. In the political world, it's about getting the most votes in an election. In the religious world, it's often about being strong enough to dominate. But the context doesn't matter. What matters is the urge of our human nature to promote ourselves and gain recognition. Even if we're not the greatest, we keep trying!

When Jesus walked with His disciples, they couldn't understand who among them was the greatest in terms of the kingdom of heaven. The religious system of their day was full of competition. People tried to follow the religious laws to look good, striving to keep every rule in the book. But no one actually could.

No one could claim to be the greatest, believing they were masters of excellence in life.

But the disciples still asked, *"Who then is greatest in the kingdom of heaven?"*

As usual, Jesus gave them a perfect answer, showing them the truth. He called a child to Himself. And as the child stood there, He told the disciples that they couldn't even enter the kingdom of heaven unless they were converted into children.

Then He added a clarification. The greatest of all the people alive would be the one who humbles himself. Humility causes a man to put himself down, be a servant, and honour others more than himself (Philippians 2:3). Will you do it?

Day Sixty-Two
THE PEOPLE JESUS CALLS

As he walked along, he saw Levi son of Alphaeus sitting at his tax collector's booth. "Follow me and be my disciple," Jesus said to him. So Levi got up and followed him.

Later, Levi invited Jesus and his disciples to his home as dinner guests, along with many tax collectors and other disreputable sinners. (There were many people of this kind among Jesus' followers.) But when the teachers of religious law who were Pharisees saw him eating with tax collectors and other sinners, they asked his disciples, "Why does he eat with such scum?"

When Jesus heard this, he told them, "Healthy people don't need a doctor—sick people do. I have come to call not those who think they are righteous, but those who know they are sinners." (Mark 2:14–17, NLT)

JESUS ENDURED A lot of criticism, and almost all of it came from the religious class. These people had nothing but disdain for Him since He didn't meet their expectations. The religious teachers of the law wouldn't associate with someone unless they carried some visual mark of religious perfection. They were only drawn to each other. Their lives never changed.

Jesus was the exact opposite. He had no urge to look for those who made Him feel special, but He always noticed the ones who were hurting, neglected, and desperate. He was always available to them. These were the ones He was drawn to, and their lives were changed.

The statement Jesus made back then is still true today: *"Healthy people don't need a doctor—sick people do. I have come to call not those who think they are righteous, but those who know they are sinners."*

What a relief it is to know that we don't have to make ourselves like the religious teachers of the law—perfect, healthy, and whole. That can take a lot of energy and still not accomplish anything of value.

The perfect expression of Jesus is only known by those who need Him: those who are sick. Likewise, the ones who hear His invitation and respond are the ones who know they are sinners in need of change.

The graciousness of Jesus is always drawn to the silent cry of the broken-hearted.

Day Sixty-Three
REMEMBER ME

For I have received of the Lord that which also I delivered unto you, that the Lord Jesus the same night in which he was betrayed took bread: and when he had given thanks, he brake it, and said, Take, eat: this is my body, which is broken for you: this do in remembrance of me. After the same manner also he took the cup, when he had supped, saying, this cup is the new testament in my blood: this do ye, as oft as ye drink it, in remembrance of me. For as often as ye eat this bread, and drink this cup, ye do shew the Lord's death till he come. Wherefore whosoever shall eat this bread, and drink this cup of the Lord, unworthily, shall be guilty of the body and blood of the Lord. But let a man examine himself, and so let him eat of that bread, and drink of that cup. (1 Corinthians 11:23–28, KJV)

JESUS DID MANY things during His time of ministry on earth, and it all had significance. Most often, his actions greatly improved people's lives. Everything He did was for the benefit of others, whether it involved turning water into wine or calling a dead young man back to life. And after performing these miracles, He never said, "Now remember who did this for you!"

As Jesus approached the end of His life on earth, He introduced His disciples to the concept of communion. While they celebrated the Passover meal, Jesus took bread and changed what it represented: *"Take, eat: this is my body, which is broken for you."* He did the same thing for the wine in the cup: *"this cup is the new testament in my blood."*

For many years, the Passover meal had been a reminder of the sacrificial lamb and the freedom their forefathers had received when God delivered them from slavery in Egypt. It helped them remember all the ways in which God had cared for them as they travelled to the Promised Land.

The words and actions of Jesus on this day must have been stunning to the disciples. He shifted their focus from the old sacrifice of long ago to Himself as the new and living sacrifice. Then He told them to break the bread and drink from the cup. This time, it wouldn't be to remember their history; it would be to remember Him. They did it well, and the church grew.

The invitation to celebrate this meal is still important for us today. The instructions were very clear: we are to do this. And as we follow His instructions and remember Him, His peace will reign in our lives.

THE PERSPECTIVE OF JESUS

> Now the tax collectors and sinners were all drawing near to hear him. And the Pharisees and the scribes grumbled, saying, "This man receives sinners and eats with them."
>
> So he told them this parable: "What man of you, having a hundred sheep, if he has lost one of them, does not leave the ninety-nine in the open country, and go after the one that is lost, until he finds it? And when he has found it, he lays it on his shoulders, rejoicing. And when he comes home, he calls together his friends and his neighbors, saying to them, 'Rejoice with me, for I have found my sheep that was lost.' Just so, I tell you, there will be more joy in heaven over one sinner who repents than over ninety-nine righteous persons who need no repentance. (Luke 15:1–7, ESV)

THE WAY JESUS lived distinguished Him from the religious elite. Those leaders chose only to associate with others like themselves. They never ate with sinners, whom they saw as unclean. They looked down on them and avoided them. The religious avoided sinners, and sinners avoided the religious.

Jesus was attracted to sinners just as they were attracted to Him. He upset the religious system and the leaders didn't like it. They grumbled amongst themselves.

But one day Jesus told a story with which they could identify. The lesson from today's passage is clear: even a shepherd goes looking for a lost sheep. He isn't focused on the ones that are safe. He focuses on the one that's lost.

Jesus was that kind of caring shepherd, looking and looking until He found the lost one. Then He carried it on His shoulders all the way home. There was no punishment for getting lost, only rejoicing over it being found.

If I'm going to live as a true Christian, following Jesus's example, I will care for the lost and hurting, carrying them home on my shoulders. I may even be found eating with them, comfortable in their presence.

It's an honour to be allowed to participate in the joy of a sinner's repentance. But that will never happen unless I'm willing to be part of the work that brought them to repentance.

Day Sixty-Five
DO YOU BELIEVE?

And as Jesus passed on from there, two blind men followed him, crying aloud, "Have mercy on us, Son of David."

When he entered the house, the blind men came to him, and Jesus said to them, "Do you believe that I am able to do this?"

They said to him, "Yes, Lord."

Then he touched their eyes, saying, "According to your faith let it be done to you."

And their eyes were opened.

And Jesus sternly warned them, "See that no one knows about it." But they went away and spread his fame through all that district. (Matthew 9:27–31, ESV)

ON A VERY busy day, a young woman touched the hem of Jesus's garment and was healed. Later that same day, He took the hand of a girl who had died and woke her up.

While this was going on, two blind men were following Him around and calling out for mercy. They kept following Him as He went into the girl's house. I wonder how long they had been following and crying out to Him before He responded?

Time wasn't a factor for the blind men; they weren't keeping track. They just wanted their eyes healed. Their faith is obvious by the fact that they kept following, even when it looked like Jesus hadn't noticed them.

Everything seems to have changed when Jesus went into the house of the dead girl. They went inside too. Now they weren't just following along with the rest of the crowd; they *"came to Him."*

And that's when Jesus responded: *"Do you believe that I am able to do this?"*

Their answer was quick. *"Yes, Lord."*

Then Jesus told them that it would be according to their faith. They were healed! Their lives were changed!

These eyes that had been blind but now saw told a story of how faith in Jesus works. Healing involves two factors: His ability and their belief. The blind men knew Him well enough to be convinced that He could heal them. That's why they kept following.

Upon being healed, we should respond the same way. And even though Jesus told them to be quiet about it, they could not be quiet. They *"spread his fame through all that district."*

When I have a life-changing encounter with Jesus, I too will spread His fame everywhere I go. Some may think it's odd, but that's just fine. His touch is real!

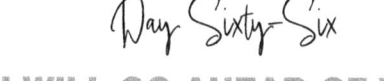

"I WILL GO AHEAD OF YOU"

After singing a hymn, they went out to the Mount of Olives.

Then Jesus told the followers, "You will all stumble in your faith, because it is written in the Scriptures: 'I will kill the shepherd, and the sheep will scatter.' But after I rise from the dead, I will go ahead of you into Galilee."

Peter said, "Everyone else may stumble in their faith, but I will not."

Jesus answered, "I tell you the truth, tonight before the rooster crows twice you will say three times you don't know me."

But Peter insisted, "I will never say that I don't know you! I will even die with you!" And all the other followers said the same thing. (Mark 14:26–31, NCV)

WE CAN EASILY be like the disciples, who enjoyed being part of what Jesus was doing. They were convinced He was the Messiah even though they didn't fully understand what that meant. In this peaceful setting on the mountain, they were sure they would stand with Jesus forever. They couldn't imagine turning their backs on Him.

Jesus knew their hearts, so their own statements didn't mean very much. He knew how they would act; self-preservation would drive them all to turn their backs on Him and walk away.

Peter didn't listen carefully to his master. He had great confidence in his opinion of himself, but no confidence in Jesus. While Jesus told him exactly what would happen, Peter argued. For some reason, on this occasion, he minimized the words of Jesus.

They must have felt very secure together on that mountain. They had learned many lessons together, but they were about to learn one of greater importance: listen closely when Jesus speaks. It's written twice in Proverbs: *"There is a way which seems right to a man, but its end is the way of death"* (Proverbs 14:12, 16:25, NASB).

The disciples learned this the hard way after they all forsook Jesus during the greatest trial of His life. Jesus passed His test and the disciples learned a lesson. From recorded history, though, it appears that they never denied Him again.

WHEN YOU PRAY

When you pray, don't be like the hypocrites. They love to stand in the synagogues and on the street corners and pray so people will see them. I tell you the truth, they already have their full reward. When you pray, you should go into your room and close the door and pray to your Father who cannot be seen. Your Father can see what is done in secret, and he will reward you.

And when you pray, don't be like those people who don't know God. They continue saying things that mean nothing, thinking that God will hear them because of their many words. Don't be like them, because your Father knows the things you need before you ask him. (Matthew 6:5–8, NCV)

WHEN JESUS WAS teaching His disciples how to pray, He knew the biggest issue would be the attitude of their hearts. That attitude was made visible in their actions.

First, Jesus talked about hypocrites. He didn't want His disciples to be like those who prayed where everyone could see and hear. Such people were only rewarded by the satisfaction of being watched and heard. They cared nothing for the presence or action of God; it was all about themselves.

Jesus wanted His disciples to be different. He instructed them to pray in a place where no one would see or hear them. They would be alone, conscious of God's presence even though they couldn't see Him. When God sees and hears these prayers given in secret, He delivers a satisfying reward.

His last lesson on prayer exposed the empty talk of those who don't even know God. They use lots of words, repeating themselves over and over, but their words have no meaning. They're just trying to convince themselves that God really cares about them.

We receive the greatest benefit when we pray in the knowledge that God cares for us and our needs. That doesn't mean we won't pray and ask for things; it just means that when we ask, we are convinced that He already knows. We don't need to pray loudly in the King James dialect. All we need to do is ask in quiet confidence. Our Father already knows.

Day Sixty-Eight
JESUS CALLS THE SINNERS

> Then it happened that as Jesus was reclining at the table in the house, behold, many tax collectors and sinners came and began dining with Jesus and His disciples.
>
> And when the Pharisees saw this, they said to His disciples, "Why is your Teacher eating with the tax collectors and sinners?"
>
> But when Jesus heard this, He said, "It is not those who are healthy who need a physician, but those who are sick. Now go and learn what this means: 'I desire compassion, rather than sacrifice,' for I did not come to call the righteous, but sinners."
> (Matthew 9:10–13, NASB)

THE TAX COLLECTORS and sinners who sat around the table eating with Jesus must have gotten a warm feeling in their hearts as they listened to Him explain the reason for their gathering.

The religious leaders avoided tax collectors and sinners, deeming them "unclean." They were afraid of being contaminated if they got too close. They couldn't understand why anyone would choose to sit at a table and eat with sinners!

Jesus taught His followers to be different. He didn't come to isolate Himself from sinners but interact with them so they could get to know Him. The more they got to know Him, the more they realized they needed Him as their Savior. He brought hope when they felt completely hopeless.

The Pharisees had to be told why Jesus did this. He made it really clear by explaining a simple principle: healthy people don't need doctors and self-righteous people don't hear when Jesus calls, but those who are sick, and those who aren't righteous, do hear Him.

Jesus didn't demand that these sinners offer sacrifices to be redeemed. He simply moved with compassion towards them. Compassion is far more powerful than condemnation. An invitation is much more welcoming than an order.

Jesus came with a heart of compassion to invite all of us sinners to know Him. Let's go out into the world and do the same.

"QUIET! BE STILL!"

That evening, Jesus said to his followers, "Let's go across the lake." Leaving the crowd behind, they took him in the boat just as he was. There were also other boats with them. A very strong wind came up on the lake. The waves came over the sides and into the boat so that it was already full of water. Jesus was at the back of the boat, sleeping with his head on a cushion. His followers woke him and said, "Teacher, don't you care that we are drowning!"

Jesus stood up and commanded the wind and said to the waves, "Quiet! Be still!" Then the wind stopped, and it became completely calm.

Jesus said to his followers, "Why are you afraid? Do you still have no faith?"

The followers were very afraid and asked each other, "Who is this? Even the wind and the waves obey him!" (Mark 4:35–41, NCV)

THE MOMENT JESUS spoke to the wind, His words changed the law of nature. It may seem as though the wind just randomly swirls around, but there are specific laws that govern when, where, and how fast the wind blows. And yet we can't see the wind.

In today's passage, when the disciples started to cross the lake, they wouldn't have had any idea that winds were about to blow and fill their boat with water. If Jesus knew what was coming, he didn't seem bothered by it. He just relaxed and went to sleep.

The storm came suddenly and the boat began filling with water. It looked to the disciples like Jesus didn't care about what was happening, but His words proved that He did care. In fact, He cared enough to take action to save them.

He stood up, fully awake and conscious of what needed to be done. He didn't try to stabilize the boat. He got to the source of the problem, which was the wind and waves. All it took was a few words from His mouth and all became peaceful. The wind and waves calmed.

Jesus's next words must have gotten to the disciples that day. They came to understand that they still had fear instead of faith, despite all they had seen Him do. It was obvious that they still didn't know who He was or what He could do.

We are like the disciples. Jesus shows us that He doesn't just stabilize the rocking boat of our lives; He calms the storm so the boat settles itself. In the process, we become acquainted with who He is and the power of His words.

IF YOU CONTINUE

So Jesus said to them, "When you lift up the Son of Man, you will know that I am he. You will know that these things I do are not by my own authority but that I say only what the Father has taught me. The One who sent me is with me. I always do what is pleasing to him, so he has not left me alone." While Jesus was saying these things, many people believed in him.

So Jesus said to the Jews who believed in him, "If you continue to obey my teaching, you are truly my followers. Then you will know the truth, and the truth will make you free." (John 8:28–32, NCV)

JESUS MADE IT very clear that everything He said was based on what His Father taught Him. Likewise, everything He did was pleasing to His Father, which is the reason God never left Him.

People must have seen evidence of this. While Jesus told everyone about His actions and relationship with His Father, they believed and trusted Him completely. For some reason, it was important for Jesus to point out that the continued presence of His Father in His life wasn't the result of some special favour. It was due to Jesus doing what was agreeable to Him, perfectly in line with His plan. This reality was the foundation of Jesus's life.

Many people believed in Jesus during His ministry, but He was looking for something more. He was looking for followers who could easily be identified; they would be the ones who continued to obey all His teachings. It wouldn't be a part-time way of life. They would live this way one hundred percent of the time, demonstrating total commitment.

These teachings of Jesus couldn't be learned from a book. We gain no freedom from trying to follow all the written rules. This freedom comes from knowing truth relationally, even though it all begins with obeying His directives.

Truth that is believed causes us to respond with obedience, but knowing the truth brings us into freedom. According to the words of Jesus, *"Then you will know the truth, and the truth will make you free."*

THE MARK OF A FOOL

Then someone called from the crowd, "Teacher, please tell my brother to divide our father's estate with me."

Jesus replied, "Friend, who made me a judge over you to decide such things as that?" Then he said, "Beware! Guard against every kind of greed. Life is not measured by how much you own."

Then he told them a story: "A rich man had a fertile farm that produced fine crops. He said to himself, 'What should I do? I don't have room for all my crops.' Then he said, 'I know! I'll tear down my barns and build bigger ones. Then I'll have room enough to store all my wheat and other goods. And I'll sit back and say to myself, 'My friend, you have enough stored away for years to come. Now take it easy! Eat, drink, and be merry!'

"But God said to him, 'You fool! You will die this very night. Then who will get everything you worked for?'

"Yes, a person is a fool to store up earthly wealth but not have a rich relationship with God." (Luke 12:13–21, NLT)

PEOPLE CAME TO Jesus for many different reasons. Many had desperate needs while others demonstrated a sense of entitlement, wanting Jesus to validate them. However, Jesus only promoted that which was valuable to His Father.

Many things in life have value because of their usefulness and necessity. The man who wanted Jesus to help him get part of his father's estate may have felt like he needed those assets to live, so he wanted the property divided into equal shares. But that didn't seem to matter to Jesus, whose life and ministry wasn't about accumulating assets or making sure everything was shared equally.

His warning is still relevant today: *"Beware! Guard against every kind of greed."* Jesus wants His followers to be driven by a higher and more profitable motivation than the accumulation of assets.

Greed is a death sentence, like being stuck in a prison of mirrors where I see myself everywhere I turn. It's impossible to have a relationship with Jesus if greed is active in our lives. But greed will be eliminated when we live as Jesus anticipated for His followers. His way is the exact opposite of greed.

This crystal-clear message from Jesus stands apart from human logic because it comes from an eternal God who proved His love for us (John 3:16). There is no greed in God.

Jesus couldn't have said it any clearer: *"Give to anyone who asks; and when things are taken away from you, don't try to get them back"* (Luke 6:30, NLT).

Only fools ignore others while making life all about themselves and their stuff.

ASK FOR WISDOM

That night God appeared to Solomon. He said, "What can I give you?"

Solomon responded to God, "You've shown great love to my father David, and you've made me king in his place. Now, Lord God, you've kept the promise you made to my father David. You've made me king of people who are as numerous as specks of dust on the ground. Give me wisdom and knowledge so that I may lead these people. After all, who can judge this great people of yours?"

God replied to Solomon, "I know this request is from your heart. You didn't ask for riches, fortunes, honor, or the death of those who hate you. You didn't even ask for a long life. Instead, you've asked for wisdom and knowledge to judge my people, over whom I made you king. So wisdom and knowledge will be given to you. I will also give you riches, fortunes, and honor like no other king before or after you." (2 Chronicles 1:7:12, GW)

SOLOMON, AND A great many others, had just finished an intense day of worship during which a thousand burnt offerings were given to God. They must have been tired after such a busy day.

That night, while Solomon slept, God asked him an important, wide-open question: *"What can I give you?"* Solomon's response showed the condition of his heart and his focus on the job ahead, showing that he knew of God's calling of his father David.

This didn't give him any sense of entitlement or special status, though. He remained focused on carefully leading the people God had called him to lead. He was aware of his job and conscious of the fact that he didn't have what he needed to do it. He asked for just one thing, something he didn't have so he could be a good king: wisdom and knowledge.

An ordinary person would have thought to ask for all sorts of things, but Solomon was different. God could see his heart, and Solomon's desire was to have something that would benefit the people more than himself.

God gave him what he asked for, plus all the other things a king would enjoy. In his life he lacked nothing.

If God were to ask what He could give you, would your answer be something that would benefit others more than yourself? We'll have no lack when our greatest desire is to have only what is needed to faithfully do the work God has placed us here to do.

Day Seventy-Three
THE CALL TO REPENT AND FOLLOW

And leaving Nazareth he went and lived in Capernaum by the sea, in the territory of Zebulun and Naphtali, so that what was spoken by the prophet Isaiah might be fulfilled: "The land of Zebulun and the land of Naphtali, the way of the sea, beyond the Jordan, Galilee of the Gentiles—the people dwelling in darkness have seen a great light, and for those dwelling in the region and shadow of death, on them a light has dawned."

From that time Jesus began to preach, saying, "Repent, for the kingdom of heaven is at hand."

While walking by the Sea of Galilee, he saw two brothers, Simon (who is called Peter) and Andrew his brother, casting a net into the sea, for they were fishermen. And he said to them, "Follow me, and I will make you fishers of men." Immediately they left their nets and followed him. And going on from there he saw two other brothers, James the son of Zebedee and John his brother, in the boat with Zebedee their father, mending their nets, and he called them. Immediately they left the boat and their father and followed him. (Matthew 4:13–22, ESV)

WHEN JESUS CALLS us to repent and follow Him, it is expected that we will make this part of our daily lives. Doing so would be life-changing, granting us a dynamic very different from the routines and expectations of people with religious titles.

The words and actions of Jesus were always perfectly coordinated. Those who watched Him could see what He was doing and believe what He said.

Jesus came to the earth to live among humans, and the light of His life called those around Him to repent. Those who did were motivated by His light. It was a normal response, leading them out of darkness and death.

While He was walking by the Sea of Galilee one day, passing among the fishermen, He called them to follow Him. This call changed their lives, giving them a whole new purpose. The call didn't come from someone whom they'd placed on a pedestal; it came from someone who walked among them. That call was so compelling that they left their boats, and their fathers, and followed Him. They didn't need time to review the implications of the decision. Something pulled at their hearts so strongly that they responded immediately.

We are called to follow Jesus and make disciples: *"Go, therefore, and make disciples of all the nations…"* (Matthew 28:19, NASB) This will require of us the same thing that was required of Jesus; we must bring light to the darkness around us, presenting examples of true followers of Christ.

GO WORK IN MY VINEYARD

The kingdom of heaven is like a person who owned some land. One morning, he went out very early to hire some people to work in his vineyard. The man agreed to pay the workers one coin for working that day. Then he sent them into the vineyard to work.

About nine o'clock the man went to the marketplace and saw some other people standing there, doing nothing. So he said to them, "If you go and work in my vineyard, I will pay you what your work is worth."

So they went to work in the vineyard.

The man went out again about twelve o'clock and three o'clock and did the same thing.

About five o'clock the man went to the marketplace again and saw others standing there. He asked them, "Why did you stand here all day doing nothing?"

They answered, "No one gave us a job."

The man said to them, "Then you can go and work in my vineyard." (Matthew 20:1–7, NCV)

JESUS ONCE TOLD a story to demonstrate what's valuable in the kingdom of heaven. It also reveals the attitude of the one who leads that kingdom, as well as the fact that there is work to be done.

In this parable, the man in charge of a vineyard goes out to find workers. These workers don't need to be highly trained; they need something to give them purpose while doing a job that needs to be done. They are also assured of a reward at the end of the day.

Throughout the day, this man finds more and more workers, calling them and promising a reward. Even when the day is almost over, he adds more workers. They have just been standing around doing nothing, since no one has given them a job to do.

Jesus came to the earth with a vision of what needed to be done in the kingdom. The workers were few and more were needed. He made this very clear to His disciples: *"The harvest is great, but the workers are few. So pray to the Lord who is in charge of the harvest; ask him to send more workers into his fields"* (Matthew 9:37–38, NLT).

If I'm aware of any emptiness in my life, it may be because I stand around idle all day, doing nothing of value in God's kingdom. But that all changes when I hear Him ask, "Why are you just standing around all day long?" His presence and attention wake me up to realize that I've been doing nothing of lasting value. When I begin to work in His vineyard, I find purpose and value.

At the end of the parable, Jesus made it clear that while it's important for us to hear the call to go work in His vineyard, the reward will come because we choose to work. No more sitting around!

Day Seventy-Five
THE BEAUTY OF THE CHOSEN

And he said to his servants, "The wedding feast is ready, and the guests I invited aren't worthy of the honor. Now go out to the street corners and invite everyone you see." So the servants brought in everyone they could find, good and bad alike, and the banquet hall was filled with guests.

But when the king came in to meet the guests, he noticed a man who wasn't wearing the proper clothes for a wedding.

"Friend," he asked, "how is it that you are here without wedding clothes?"

But the man had no reply.

Then the king said to his aides, "Bind his hands and feet and throw him into the outer darkness, where there will be weeping and gnashing of teeth."

For many are called, but few are chosen. (Matthew 22:8–14, NLT)

THE WORDS OF this parable are as significant for us today as they were when Jesus first spoke them. Human nature hasn't changed, nor have God's expectations. Changes in our culture over time have no influence in the kingdom of heaven, so we should learn the importance of those things that are eternal. This will keep us from deception and disappointment.

In the first part of this story (Matthew 22:1–7), a man invited many people to a wedding feast. These entitled friends react with disrespect. Therefore, the man has his servants invite anyone they encounter on the street. These people didn't have any connection to the family at all. They were invited just as they were, the good and the bad.

So they all came, dressed for the wedding.

But one man obviously hadn't thought it was important to dress for the occasion. He came in his street clothes—and that attitude cost him everything.

The lesson Jesus wanted to impart is simple: it's important to be called, since one needs an invitation to attend a ceremony, but one must be chosen in order to remain at the feast. In other words, everyone is invited but those chosen to remain are those who transform from strangers on the street to participants in the family.

We simply let Him do to us what's necessary to change our lives.

> I will rejoice greatly in the Lord, my soul will be joyful in my God; for He has clothed me with garments of salvation, He has wrapped me with a robe of righteousness, as a groom puts on a turban, and as a bride adorns herself with her jewels. (Isaiah 61:10, NASB)

We can only come as we are, but we can't stay as we are. God wants to change us.

IT'S ALL ABOUT THE HEART

> And He said to them, "Are you so lacking in understanding as well? Do you not understand that whatever goes into the person from outside cannot defile him, because it does not go into his heart, but into his stomach, and is eliminated?" (Thereby He declared all foods clean.) And He was saying, "That which comes out of the person, that is what defiles the person. For from within, out of the hearts of people, come the evil thoughts, acts of sexual immorality, thefts, murders, acts of adultery, deeds of greed, wickedness, deceit, indecent behavior, envy, slander, pride, and foolishness. All these evil things come from within and defile the person."
> (Mark 7:18–23, NASB)

MANY OF THE religious rules of Jesus's day had no value because they did nothing to improve the character, or safety, of those who followed the rules. Jesus upset the religious leaders and turned their world upside-down by pointing out the real problem: people will always find ways to express the true desires of their hearts.

Since the beginning of time, our human nature has caused us to defend ourselves by blaming our poor behaviours on others. Adam blamed his wife, and his wife blamed the serpent. The actual driving force behind their actions was their desire for something that didn't belong to them—and God held them accountable.

God knew how this would end unless a new path was forged. The people of Israel often blamed their wrongdoings on the heathen nations around them, but God knew the truth. That's why He promised to bring change:

> Then I will sprinkle clean water on you, and you will be clean; I will cleanse you from all your filthiness and from all your idols. Moreover, I will give you a new heart and put a new spirit within you; and I will remove the heart of stone from your flesh and give you a heart of flesh. And I will put My Spirit within you and bring it about that you walk in My statutes, and are careful and follow My ordinances. (Ezekiel 36:25–27, NASB)

Jesus opened the way for us to have clean, new hearts (1 John 1:9), fulfilling the promise God gave Ezekiel to change the motivations that drive our actions.

The actions of my life will always be an expression of the condition of my heart.

Day Seventy-Seven
"WHO DO YOU SAY I AM?"

Jesus went out, along with His disciples, to the villages of Caesarea Philippi; and on the way He questioned His disciples, saying to them, "Who do people say that I am?"

They told Him, saying, "John the Baptist; and others say Elijah; and others, one of the prophets."

And He continued questioning them: "But who do you say that I am?"

Peter answered and said to Him, "You are the Christ."

And He warned them to tell no one about Him. And He began to teach them that the Son of Man must suffer many things and be rejected by the elders and the chief priests and the scribes, and be killed, and after three days rise from the dead. (Mark 8:27–31, NASB)

WHEN JESUS ASKED His disciples a question, He wasn't looking for information. He already knew what people thought about Him, and who they thought He was. The reason He asked these questions was to increase the disciples' own awareness. They needed to know how others identified Jesus.

But the most important question related to how the disciples identified Him.

Some thought He was the second coming of John the Baptist. Others thought He was a prophet of old. Amazingly, the prophets were the ones who had prophesied that someone else would come and be the Messiah. Those prophets had never made their foretellings about themselves.

Many people watched Jesus and noticed that many of His actions resembled all these prophecies they had heard before. While they knew some things about Him, they didn't know *Him*. This made it impossible for them to identify Him as the Christ.

The disciples had lived with Him and knew Him well enough to know that He was the Christ, the appointed and anointed Messiah. There was no question about it. However, this knowledge didn't keep them from running for their lives when Jesus was crucified. They had only seen a part of what the Messiah would be like. They didn't appreciate the full expression that was yet to come. They would see it soon, though, and it would change their lives.

Jesus tried to show them a fuller picture of who He was. He taught them that He was the Son of Man who would suffer, be killed, and then be raised back to life after three days. Peter, and probably the rest of the disciples, couldn't compute this. He even tried to correct Jesus.

He was the Christ and Son of Man at the same time. This qualified Him to be and do the work to become our Redeemer. Now we can be saved because of Him.

Day Seventy-Eight
THE DANGER OF TRADITIONS

The Pharisees and some of the scribes gathered to Him after they came from Jerusalem, and saw that some of His disciples were eating their bread with unholy hands, that is, unwashed. (For the Pharisees and all the other Jews do not eat unless they carefully wash their hands, thereby holding firmly to the tradition of the elders; and when they come from the marketplace, they do not eat unless they completely cleanse themselves; and there are many other things which they have received as traditions to firmly hold, such as the washing of cups, pitchers, and copper pots.)

And the Pharisees and the scribes asked Him, "Why do Your disciples not walk in accordance with the tradition of the elders, but eat their bread with unholy hands?"

But He said to them, "Rightly did Isaiah prophesy about you hypocrites, as it is written: 'This people honors Me with their lips, but their heart is far away from Me. And in vain do they worship Me, teaching as doctrines the commandments of men.' Neglecting the commandment of God, you hold to the tradition of men." He was also saying to them, "You are experts at setting aside the commandment of God in order to keep your tradition." (Mark 7:1–9, NASB)

IN THIS PASSAGE, we read that the scribes and Pharisees couldn't understand how the disciples of Jesus could violate such a long-standing law. That had been enforced by the highest council in Israel and needed to be obeyed.

Laws like this hadn't been written down by Moses or any of the prophets. They were passed down orally through past generations. It can be assumed that some highly esteemed religious figure had made these rules, and they had stuck.

Obedience to rules of tradition has a different effect on us than obedience to the commands of God. When Jesus said that their worship was in vain, it didn't just mean that the act was empty and useless; it meant that they were prioritizing their extremely high opinion of themselves over worshipping and obeying God. They lacked relationship and their emptiness drove them to talk a lot and point out the faults of others.

God desires relationship with us. All His instructions are meant to build a working relationship between us and Him. If we add anything to these instructions, we weaken our relationship with God.

As Titus 1:16 tells us, *"They profess to know God, but by their deeds they deny Him, being detestable and disobedient and worthless for any good deed"* (NASB).

Our lives are made fulfilling when we simply do what He says to do. All the things we do declare that we know Him, freeing us from having to use lots of words to pretend to honour Him. He will be honoured by the lives we live.

Day Seventy-Nine
CHOOSE LIKE GOD CHOOSES

For the foolishness of God is wiser than mankind, and the weakness of God is stronger than mankind.

For consider your calling, brothers and sisters, that there were not many wise according to the flesh, not many mighty, not many noble; but God has chosen the foolish things of the world to shame the wise, and God has chosen the weak things of the world to shame the things which are strong, and the insignificant things of the world and the despised God has chosen, the things that are not, so that He may nullify the things that are, so that no human may boast before God. But it is due to Him that you are in Christ Jesus, who became to us wisdom from God, and righteousness and sanctification, and redemption, so that, just as it is written: "Let the one who boasts, boast in the Lord." (1 Corinthians 1:25–31, NASB)

MAKING DECISIONS IS part of life. We make so many choices in a day that we most often do it without thinking. In fact, studies indicate that we make more than thirty thousand decisions per day. If this is correct, and we subtract time for sleeping, we average one decision every other second—and most of these choices are made subconsciously.

What is the real driver behind our decision-making? Do we even care about what drives us? What would it be like if we cared about every individual decision?

God certainly makes lots of choices, and He cares about each one. They all have a definite purpose: *"so that no human may boast before God."*

Human nature is very predictable. We like to present ourselves as being wiser, stronger, and culturally superior to others. There's nothing humble in this way of thinking. It's all about self-promotion and boasting.

But this all changes after we wake up and have an encounter with God's Son, Jesus Christ. In the process of becoming acquainted with Him and His touch, our every motivation shifts, influencing every choice we make. The dominant factor is no longer ego but rather His glory.

According to 2 Corinthians 10:17–18, *"But the one who boasts is to boast in the Lord. For it is not the one who commends himself that is approved, but the one whom the Lord commends"* (NASB).

When Jesus reaches out and touches our lives, we receive the greatest possible honour. This is the work of God and cannot be duplicated by anything else.

Day Eighty
THE ACTIONS OF A WISE MAN

Not everyone who says to me, "Lord, Lord," will enter the kingdom of heaven, but the one who does the will of my Father who is in heaven. On that day many will say to me, "Lord, Lord, did we not prophesy in your name, and cast out demons in your name, and do many mighty works in your name?" And then will I declare to them, "I never knew you; depart from me, you workers of lawlessness."

Everyone then who hears these words of mine and does them will be like a wise man who built his house on the rock. And the rain fell, and the floods came, and the winds blew and beat on that house, but it did not fall, because it had been founded on the rock. And everyone who hears these words of mine and does not do them will be like a foolish man who built his house on the sand. And the rain fell, and the floods came, and the winds blew and beat against that house, and it fell, and great was the fall of it. (Matthew 7:21–27, ESV)

ONE OF THE first indications that a man is wise is that he is open to instructions. He also has the ability to follow instructions, knowing there are other people smarter than himself. Wise people learn from other people's failures and successes.

Jesus knew that many people would talk, saying the right words without listening and following instructions. Without the ability to listen and follow His instructions, though, it's impossible to enjoy life in the kingdom of heaven.

He pointed out the disappointment many would feel, thinking they had qualified for entry on account of the good things they'd done. They may have used the name of Jesus, but they had no relationship with Him. They lacked communication with God and never knew what He wanted. They assumed their knowledge of His past actions could direct their current actions. But their lack of relationship caused them to act without direction. They were lawless.

Jesus speaks very clearly about those who hear His words and do them. Such men are wise. It's not so much that they know everything but that they recognize His instructions and follow them, leading to success.

Wisdom is found in those with open ears. Wise ones are confident that He knows everything—past, present, and future—and that His words are perfect. They trust Him completely, and this trust motivates them to follow His instructions. Not even the greatest storm could bring them down.

Those who are foolish hear His words but instead trust themselves, discarding wisdom. The consequences are devastating, for everything they do is destroyed.

Wisdom isn't proven by words. As Matthew 7 teaches, it's proven by winds.

GO FOR WHAT'S COMPLETE

And someone came to Him and said, "Teacher, what good thing shall I do so that I may obtain eternal life?"

And He said to him, "Why are you asking Me about what is good? There is only One who is good; but if you want to enter life, keep the commandments."

Then he said to Him, "Which ones?"

And Jesus said, "You shall not commit murder; You shall not commit adultery; You shall not steal; You shall not give false testimony; Honor your father and mother; and You shall love your neighbor as yourself."

The young man said to Him, "All these I have kept; what am I still lacking?"

Jesus said to him, "If you want to be complete, go and sell your possessions and give to the poor, and you will have treasure in heaven; and come, follow Me."

But when the young man heard this statement, he went away grieving; for he was one who owned much property. (Matthew 19:16–22, NASB)

WHEN SOMEONE ASKED Jesus a question, He always got right to the heart of the issue. In this passage, the young man wanted to know what "good thing" he needed to do in order to have a life that would last. This "good thing" would be something that benefited him. He just didn't know what it was, or what it would take to get it.

Jesus started by explaining that life can be good by simply keeping the commandments. This keeps people around safe, because it means they won't be harmed. Neither will anyone carry guilt or condemnation.

But the man was looking for something of greater benefit than that. He had been keeping all the commandments already and wasn't seeing results. He wanted to find out what he was lacking, for he knew he was missing something. His life wasn't full. He was hungry for a more satisfying life.

The answer Jesus gave him tore at his heart. Jesus knew this young man had great possessions. The problem, though, was that his possessions possessed him. When the man realized he couldn't do the one thing he needed to do—get rid of his possessions—he went away greatly distressed and sad.

I too can have a full life when nothing I have possesses me. Everything I have belongs to Jesus.

Day Eighty-Two
"TOUCH ME AND SEE"

Now while they were telling these things, Jesus Himself suddenly stood in their midst and said to them, "Peace be to you."

But they were startled and frightened, and thought that they were looking at a spirit.

And He said to them, "Why are you frightened, and why are doubts arising in your hearts? See My hands and My feet, that it is I Myself; touch Me and see, because a spirit does not have flesh and bones as you plainly see that I have."

And when He had said this, He showed them His hands and His feet. While they still could not believe it because of their joy and astonishment, He said to them, "Have you anything here to eat?"

They served Him a piece of broiled fish; and He took it and ate it in front of them. (Luke 24:36–43, NASB)

OUR MOST UNEXPECTED and unusual experiences can very quickly overwhelm our sense of stability. The peaceful, normal routine can be replaced by these unexpected and unexplainable events. Our brains struggle to explain this, but the answer is elusive. Fear and doubt can dominate our emotions.

This is exactly what happened when Jesus appeared to the disciples after His crucifixion and told them to be at peace. It was a nice greeting, to be sure, but they couldn't believe their eyes and ears. The sight of him was totally out of alignment with their expectations. They were perplexed and couldn't deal with their doubt.

Jesus could see their fear and doubt and, thankfully, had the perfect way to bring peace and stability amidst their chaos. He said, very simply, *"Touch Me and see."* They still had a hard time believing that it was really Him, but soon their emotions turned to joy and amazement. He had returned, just like He had said He would. There could be no more doubt.

In our world, with all our disappointments and unexpected perplexities, is it possible for us to go through troubles and come out the other side filled with joy and amazement? Yes! For this reason: *"Jesus Christ the same yesterday, and to day, and for ever"* (Hebrews 13:8, KJV).

After reintroducing Himself to His disciples, they shared some fish with Him and He ate. They enjoyed His presence—and so can we!

Day Eighty-Three
KNOW WHAT'S IMPORTANT

Which of you by worrying can add one cubit to his stature?

So why do you worry about clothing? Consider the lilies of the field, how they grow: they neither toil nor spin; and yet I say to you that even Solomon in all his glory was not arrayed like one of these. Now if God so clothes the grass of the field, which today is, and tomorrow is thrown into the oven, will He not much more clothe you, O you of little faith?

Therefore do not worry, saying, "What shall we eat?" or "What shall we drink?" or "What shall we wear?" For after all these things the Gentiles seek. For your heavenly Father knows that you need all these things. But seek first the kingdom of God and His righteousness, and all these things shall be added to you. (Matthew 6:27–33, NKJV)

JESUS BROUGHT AN eternal perspective whenever He taught. While teaching His disciples one day, He asked, *"Which of you by worrying can add one cubit to his stature?"* They must have wondered who would ever worry about trying to add a cubit (about eighteen inches) to their height. That would be a very unusual thing to do.

No, they didn't worry about getting taller, nor did they know anyone who did. Obviously being worried can't add to one's height.

He then asked another question: *"So why do you worry about clothing?"* His point was clear: worry and anxiety can't produce anything.

Jesus knew that God created and cares for all things. God knows how to give the flowers everything they need to be complete and beautiful. And if He cares for the flowers so perfectly, Jesus pointed out, wouldn't He take care of us too?

When I know this is true, I don't worry about anything, whether it's food, water, or clothes. My heavenly Father who cares about me, knows everything, and gives me all I need. I feel hungry to pursue God and His character, things of eternal significance.

My heavenly Father will give me everything I need.

Day Eighty-Four
A BIG WHY QUESTION

Why do you notice the little piece of dust in your friend's eye, but you don't notice the big piece of wood in your own eye? How can you say to your friend, "Friend, let me take that little piece of dust out of your eye" when you cannot see that big piece of wood in your own eye! You hypocrite! First, take the wood out of your own eye. Then you will see clearly to take the dust out of your friend's eye.

A good tree does not produce bad fruit, nor does a bad tree produce good fruit. Each tree is known by its own fruit. People don't gather figs from thornbushes, and they don't get grapes from bushes. (Luke 6:41–44, NCV)

IN THIS PASSAGE, Jesus asked a very interesting question. Why would I notice a piece of dust in my friend's eye? It would hardly be noticeable. His eye might water a bit, but otherwise it would be hard to see.

The big piece of wood in my own eye would be very easy to see. In fact, everyone would notice it.

The disciples didn't wonder about *how* to see the speck in a friend's eye, but rather *why* it was visible. And *why* would a person fail to see the huge piece of wood in their own eye? If we can only resolve this problem, we'll no longer view the world through a view cluttered with garbage.

Our relationships with others are only as good as the relationship we have with ourselves. And if we have an authentic relationship with

Jesus, we will naturally be authentic with others. We won't overlook the wood in our own eyes because we see the uncluttered beauty of our Good Shepherd, not to mention the true value of our friends. We will demonstrate no hypocrisy. We will help each other stay clean because we choose to see ourselves clearly.

When we are made clean, we don't leave a dirty mark on everything we touch. After all, only a good tree can produce good fruit, and a bad tree can only produce bad fruit.

Many people look for relationships that strengthen and encourage them. They don't approach those who choose to ignore the chunk of wood in their own eyes. Such people can't be trusted.

Why would I refuse to deal with the chunk of wood in my eye?

Day Eighty-Five
THE MARK OF A TRUTHFUL PERSON

Jesus said to them, "If God were your Father, you would love Me, for I proceeded forth and came from God; nor have I come of Myself, but He sent Me. Why do you not understand My speech? Because you are not able to listen to My word. You are of your father the devil, and the desires of your father you want to do. He was a murderer from the beginning, and does not stand in the truth, because there is no truth in him. When he speaks a lie, he speaks from his own resources, for he is a liar and the father of it. But because I tell the truth, you do not believe Me. Which of you convicts Me of sin? And if I tell the truth, why do you not believe Me? He who is of God hears God's words; therefore you do not hear, because you are not of God."

Then the Jews answered and said to Him, "Do we not say rightly that You are a Samaritan and have a demon?"

Jesus answered, "I do not have a demon; but I honor My Father, and you dishonor Me. And I do not seek My own glory; there is One who seeks and judges." (John 8:42–50, NKJV)

AS JESUS SPOKE to the Pharisees, they challenged Him about who He really was. They couldn't comprehend that God had sent Him as the Messiah. They criticized Him for almost everything He said, having no idea who He was, where He came from, or the identity of His Father.

Jesus's life was anchored in a way theirs weren't, causing them to see things differently. Their lives were self-involved; His revolved around His Father. They couldn't understand His speech because they didn't have the ability to hear His word. They had come to kill Him, but He had come to save them. Their outlooks were opposite to each other.

Today, my view of Him determines how I relate to the words of Jesus. If I see the expression of God in His life, I will believe and follow Him. His words will change my life. This is about more than reading something from the pages of a book; it's about connecting to the divine expression of God, which leaves a visible mark on everything I do.

Jesus said, *"I honor my Father… I do not seek My own glory."* All followers of Jesus can say the same. Just as this validated the life of Jesus, it validates my life as well.

Day Eighty-Six
GIVE TO GOD WHAT BELONGS TO GOD

Then the Pharisees met together to plot how to trap Jesus into saying something for which he could be arrested. They sent some of their disciples, along with the supporters of Herod, to meet with him.

"Teacher," they said, "we know how honest you are. You teach the way of God truthfully. You are impartial and don't play favorites. Now tell us what you think about this: Is it right to pay taxes to Caesar or not?"

But Jesus knew their evil motives. "You hypocrites!" he said. "Why are you trying to trap me? Here, show me the coin used for the tax." When they handed him a Roman coin, he asked, "Whose picture and title are stamped on it?"

"Caesar's," they replied.

"Well, then," he said, "give to Caesar what belongs to Caesar, and give to God what belongs to God."

His reply amazed them, and they went away. (Matthew 22:15–22, NLT)

JESUS WAS ALWAYS honest and open about His life because He wanted everyone to see and share the beautiful relationship He had with His Father. Everything He did pointed to His Father, motivating large crowds to follow Him.

But the Pharisees had a problem, because they were the exact opposite. They wanted the people to see *them*, and so their every action pointed to themselves. Since they had nothing valuable to share, few followed in their footsteps.

This difference drove the Pharisees to look for ways to get rid of Him. They thought they could use His opinion of governmental tax laws to incriminate Him. But instead they received some unexpected teaching.

The Roman Empire funded itself in a very common way, by registering all births and requiring its citizens to pay tax. This system is what resulted in Mary and Joseph travelling to Bethlehem at the time of Jesus's birth.

Many years earlier, God had revealed through a prophet that the Messiah would be born in Bethlehem (Micah 5:2). So Jesus would have been aware that God could use even tax laws for His benefit, motivating Mary and Joseph to travel there. Jesus could always put things in a heavenly perspective.

He pointed out to the Pharisees how simple it was to recognize that which belonged to Caesar: it had his mark on it. All they had to do was give to Caesar what belonged to him.

Jesus didn't stop there, though, adding: *"and give to God what belongs to God."*

We can recognize what belongs to God in the same way: it has His mark on it. We honour God by giving Him everything that belongs to Him, keeping none of it for ourselves.

Day Eighty-Seven
FORGIVENESS OPENS THE DOOR TO LOVE

So Jesus said, "Two men owed a moneylender some money. One owed him five hundred silver coins, and the other owed him fifty. When they couldn't pay it back, he was kind enough to cancel their debts. Now, who do you think will love him the most?"

Simon answered, "I suppose the one who had the largest debt canceled."

Jesus said to him, "You're right!" Then, turning to the woman, he said to Simon, "You see this woman, don't you? I came into your house. You didn't wash my feet. But she has washed my feet with her tears and dried them with her hair. You didn't give me a kiss. But ever since I came in, she has not stopped kissing my feet. You didn't put any olive oil on my head. But she has poured perfume on my feet. That's why I'm telling you that her many sins have been forgiven. Her great love proves that. But whoever receives little forgiveness loves very little."
(Luke 7:41–47, GW)

JESUS HAD BEEN invited to the home of a Pharisee for a meal. Soon after He was seated, a woman entered and began to cry, using her tears to wash His feet, then wiping them dry with her hair. With overflowing love, she kissed His feet and anointed them with a very costly perfume.

Jesus's host, Simon, was a bit startled. He concluded that Jesus wasn't much of a prophet, since He couldn't tell that this woman touching Him was sinful. In reality, Jesus was more than a prophet and taught this Pharisee some important lessons about love and forgiveness.

He wanted Simon to understand why some show greater love than others. The answer was directly connected to how much a person had been forgiven. This woman knew she had been forgiven for a great debt, while Simon knew very little forgiveness. Her love for Him was therefore much more obvious.

Could it be that a lack of love expressed by professed Christians demonstrates that they don't know their own forgiveness?

When I only recognize a small amount of forgiveness, I see myself as being pretty good and thus have a limited capacity to love, just like Simon the Pharisee. But my love for Jesus and others will be unlimited when I recognize the great amount of forgiveness I have received from Jesus. He died on an old rugged cross to forgive me of my awful sins. Now love flows freely.

Day Eighty-Eight
ACTIONS IN HONOUR OF JESUS

Now when Jesus was in Bethany, at the home of Simon the Leper, a woman came to Him with an alabaster vial of very expensive perfume, and she poured it on His head as He was reclining at the table.

But the disciples were indignant when they saw this, and said, "Why this waste? For this perfume could have been sold for a high price and the money given to the poor."

But Jesus, aware of this, said to them, "Why are you bothering the woman? For she has done a good deed for Me. For you always have the poor with you; but you do not always have Me. For when she poured this perfume on My body, she did it to prepare Me for burial. Truly I say to you, wherever this gospel is preached in the whole world, what this woman has done will also be told in memory of her."
(Matthew 26:6–13, NASB)

SOME OF THE most significant events happen when we're just going about our routines. We can feel their importance. But when we see such things happen to others, it's much easier to brush it off.

The woman in this story, Mary, not only anointed His head but also His feet (John 12:1–8). She sat at His feet and listened to Him speak while her sister Martha busied herself in the kitchen (Luke 10:40–42).

Know that there's nothing wrong with choosing to work, but making the choice to sit and listen can give us a life-changing perspective. This is exactly what it did for Mary.

Mary's perfume was expensive and she paid a great price for it, knowing it would be used for a great purpose for someone she loved. She may not have perfectly understood everything that would soon happen to Jesus, but God did. Jesus was being prepared to die.

When Jesus noticed that the disciples were annoyed with Mary, they probably got very quiet. He had to explain to them what was really happening. He didn't minimize the importance of helping the poor; His words were meant to recognize the beauty of what had just happened.

Mary had honoured Jesus in an extreme way, and her perfect actions prepared Jesus for His upcoming burial. And amazingly, the disciples criticized her!

Is it possible that we too may be criticized for the honour we give to Jesus? We will never be able to rightly honour the poor if we don't give the first honour to Jesus.

Day Eighty-Nine
WATCH OUT FOR THE WRONG BREAD

And leaving them, He again embarked and went away to the other side.

And the disciples had forgotten to take bread, and did not have more than one loaf in the boat with them. And He was giving orders to them, saying, "Watch out! Beware of the leaven of the Pharisees, and the leaven of Herod."

And they began to discuss with one another the fact that they had no bread.

And Jesus, aware of this, said to them, "Why are you discussing the fact that you have no bread? Do you not yet comprehend or understand? Do you still have your heart hardened? Having eyes, do you not see? And having ears, do you not hear? And do you not remember, when I broke the five loaves for the five thousand, how many baskets full of broken pieces you picked up?"

They said to Him, "Twelve."

"When I broke the seven for the four thousand, how many large baskets full of broken pieces did you pick up?"

And they said to Him, "Seven."

And He was saying to them, "Do you not yet understand?" (Mark 8:13–21, NASB)

IN MARK 8, Jesus used some words of warning to get the disciples' attention, alerting them that danger was close. He warned them to watch for something in the hearts of the Pharisees, as well as King Herod, that would cause great difficulty for His followers.

But something in the disciples' own hearts caused them to miss the warning. They instead focused on their own lack of physical bread.

Jesus had to remind them that physical bread, which nourishes the body, doesn't present an issue. He could multiply a few loaves to feed thousands and have some leftover. They remembered this miracle well.

However, Jesus was talking about another kind of bread, one that didn't come from Him. This bread wouldn't nurture the physical body but rather feed and motivate people's souls towards self-righteousness.

Jesus was concerned that His disciples lacked understanding of His warning.

To understand Jesus, we must have a good relationship with Him. With this understanding, we will choose the right bread.

Day Ninety
THE TRUE BREAD

They answered, "Show us a miraculous sign if you want us to believe in you. What can you do? After all, our ancestors ate manna while they journeyed through the wilderness! The Scriptures say, 'Moses gave them bread from heaven to eat.'"

Jesus said, "I tell you the truth, Moses didn't give you bread from heaven. My Father did. And now he offers you the true bread from heaven. The true bread of God is the one who comes down from heaven and gives life to the world."

"Sir," they said, "give us that bread every day."

Jesus replied, "I am the bread of life. Whoever comes to me will never be hungry again. Whoever believes in me will never be thirsty." (John 6:30–35, NLT)

WHILE TEACHING, JESUS was confronted by those who challenged His authority. The Jews compared Him to different figures from their history, thinking of them more as idols than servants of God. This made it impossible for them to see Jesus for who He was. In order to believe, they needed some miraculous sign.

They thought Moses had been the one to give them manna in the wilderness. Jesus had to correct their thinking. They may have been shocked when Jesus said, *"I tell you the truth, Moses didn't give you bread from heaven. My Father did."*

Jesus went on to explain that His Father was taking the provision of bread to a whole new level. The benefit of this spiritual bread far exceeded that of manna in the wilderness.

Even though God provided both types of bread, the manna spoiled after twenty-four hours. His spiritual bread was eternal.

The people listening to Him that day were very interested in this new bread, especially when they heard that it would give life to the world. They wanted it immediately!

However, they changed their minds when they heard that this bread was the person of Jesus. They couldn't believe it.

> Then the people began to murmur in disagreement because he had said, "I am the bread that came down from heaven." They said, "Isn't this Jesus, the son of Joseph? We know his father and mother. How can he say, 'I came down from heaven'?" (John 6:41–42, NLT)

When I know Jesus as the bread sent by God, He will satisfy every hunger and thirst in my life. There is no greater satisfaction than coming to Jesus and enjoying the true Bread.

Day Ninety-One
A NEW NAME

When Abram was ninety-nine years old, the Lord appeared to him and said, "I am El-Shaddai—'God Almighty.' Serve me faithfully and live a blameless life. I will make a covenant with you, by which I will guarantee to give you countless descendants."

At this, Abram fell face down on the ground. Then God said to him, "This is my covenant with you: I will make you the father of a multitude of nations! What's more, I am changing your name. It will no longer be Abram. Instead, you will be called Abraham, for you will be the father of many nations. I will make you extremely fruitful. Your descendants will become many nations, and kings will be among them!

"I will confirm my covenant with you and your descendants after you, from generation to generation. This is the everlasting covenant: I will always be your God and the God of your descendants after you. And I will give the entire land of Canaan, where you now live as a foreigner, to you and your descendants. It will be their possession forever, and I will be their God." (Genesis 17:1–8, NLT)

WHEN SOMEONE HAS a direct encounter with God, they don't walk away the same. There will be a change.

Abram was no different. The unexpected encounter in this passage left him facedown on the ground, overpowered by the revelation of God.

Earlier, he'd met with God and heard His promise of a son. But when it didn't seem to work out, he and his wife made some arrangements for him to have a child with a servant.

Ishmeal was born and Abram loved him, believing he was the son God had promised. Abram was a good father and the people around him must have noticed how he treated his only son. But since this wasn't the son God had intended, a change needed to occur to set the stage for Isaac's appearance. Abram would need a different mindset.

When God started talking to Abram, He made a promise, guaranteeing him many descendants, including many nations and kings. This would happen over many generations. His name would need to be changed, though. Names are important because they speak of our character. The meaning of Abram's name changed from "exalted father" to "father of a multitude." After being known as Abraham, he became an honourable father of many, not just one son.

God still works that way today. He makes changes in our lives to produce the character in us He wants to see. Only then can we do perfectly what He wants us to do.

Day Ninety-Two
GOD IS DOING SOMETHING NEW

I am the Lord, your Holy One, Israel's Creator and King. I am the Lord, who opened a way through the waters, making a dry path through the sea. I called forth the mighty army of Egypt with all its chariots and horses. I drew them beneath the waves, and they drowned, their lives snuffed out like a smoldering candlewick.

But forget all that—it is nothing compared to what I am going to do. For I am about to do something new. See, I have already begun! Do you not see it? I will make a pathway through the wilderness. I will create rivers in the dry wasteland. (Isaiah 43:15–19, NLT)

GOD WANTS US to get to know Him by watching Him—because when we can see what He's doing, it's easier for us to understand what He wants us to do.

We often try to discover what God wants from us by trying to figure out what He likes. This mentality drives us to write rules of conduct and harshly judge those who don't follow the rules. This never produces a relationship with God, because the image of Him in our minds blocks our view of reality. It's like standing in the shadow of a huge idol, blocking out the sun.

Thankfully, our God isn't built with wood or stone. He has always been alive and active. As we watch and learn, we easily see the things He has already done in the past, things that are finished. Then there are the things He does in the present. But there are also things

He will yet do in the future. These actions can trouble us if we aren't connected well enough to understand what motivates Him.

There is a purpose for everything God does, as well as a process to accomplish that purpose. While the process will change from time to time, the purpose is consistent. When I understand the purpose, the reason for God's actions, I can remain untroubled when He starts doing something new.

Our human nature finds security in consistency, from everything staying the same and never changing. This doesn't bring freedom; it just keeps the prison doors locked.

Let's wake up! God always does what He says, and He is about to do something new! In fact, He has already begun to do it. Of all the wonderful things He has done for us in the past, these new things will outshine them all.

Day Ninety-Three
RESTING AFTER RETURNING

This is what the Sovereign Lord, the Holy One of Israel, says: "Only in returning to me and resting in me will you be saved. In quietness and confidence is your strength. But you would have none of it. You said, 'No, we will get our help from Egypt. They will give us swift horses for riding into battle.' But the only swiftness you are going to see is the swiftness of your enemies chasing you! One of them will chase a thousand of you. Five of them will make all of you flee. You will be left like a lonely flagpole on a hill or a tattered banner on a distant mountaintop."

So the Lord must wait for you to come to him so he can show you his love and compassion. For the Lord is a faithful God. Blessed are those who wait for his help. (Isaiah 30:15–18, NLT)

THE WORDS OF God are always clear and understandable when we're connected to Him in a relational way. That's why God gave Israel this crucial first step: to return to Him and stay. God is our only place of safety, where our confidence in Him silences our anxious inner voices.

Israel found it difficult to approach a God they couldn't see, so they chose something they could see: fast, beautiful horses. But these horses couldn't give them what they needed. Though a person may think he has the fastest horse, someone else's will probably be faster.

God warned His people by giving them a glimpse at how their lives would end up. He showed them that they'd end up like a lonely flagpole on a remote hill, never to be used again.

But God wouldn't turn His back on them. He waited for them, and now for us, for a simple reason: He wants us to experience His love and compassion. These are the most compelling actions of God. I can hear His words and listen, but my heart is gripped when I see His love and I'm convinced that He cares for me. His love and compassion silence the inner voices directing me to run for safety.

Our world today is fast-paced, always moving toward something new, sometimes something safer or more profitable. Through this process of trying to keep up with everything, we forfeit our ability to simply wait.

It's hard to sit and quietly wait. The only way is to return to Him. He is waiting perfectly and will teach us how to do the same.

Day Ninety-Four
WHAT ARE YOU SEEKING?

"And I have seen and have borne witness that this is the Son of God."

The next day again John was standing with two of his disciples, and he looked at Jesus as he walked by and said, "Behold, the Lamb of God!"

The two disciples heard him say this, and they followed Jesus.

Jesus turned and saw them following and said to them, "What are you seeking?"

And they said to him, "Rabbi" (which means Teacher), "where are you staying?"

He said to them, "Come and you will see."

So they came and saw where he was staying, and they stayed with him that day, for it was about the tenth hour. One of the two who heard John speak and followed Jesus was Andrew, Simon Peter's brother. He first found his own brother Simon and said to him, "We have found the Messiah" (which means Christ). (John 1:34–41, ESV)

IF YOU COULD define your most important goal in life, what would it be? It's important to know what motivates our actions, whether or not we're aware of it.

John the Baptist had two disciples who became aware that Jesus was the Messiah, the Lamb of God. When they saw Him and discovered who He was, they started following Him immediately. They didn't ask whether it was okay. They didn't talk about it. They just followed. They knew what they wanted most.

When Jesus noticed these men were following Him, He wasn't interested in finding out who they were or who had sent them. He merely asked a simple question: *"What are you seeking?"* This intense question was meant to expose what they really wanted.

Their answer may sound surprising. They weren't looking for a dramatic sign to prove who Jesus was; they only wanted to see where Jesus stayed. They were interested in where He lived, as this would reveal a great deal about His character.

Jesus invited them in. Once they'd seen the place and stayed a while, they came back and announced, *"We have found the Messiah."* They confirmed who He was when they spent time with Him, in the place where He lived. It changed their lives.

There are many ways by which we can be introduced to Jesus, and many reasons for which we will want to follow Him. But our greatest delight will come when He invites us to come and see Him in the place He consistently lives.

Day Ninety-Five
DIVINE INSTRUCTIONS

> Light exposes the true character of everything because light makes everything easy to see. That's why it says: "Wake up, sleeper! Rise from the dead, and Christ will shine on you." So then, be very careful how you live. Don't live like foolish people but like wise people. Make the most of your opportunities because these are evil days. So don't be foolish, but understand what the Lord wants. Don't get drunk on wine, which leads to wild living. Instead, be filled with the Spirit by reciting psalms, hymns, and spiritual songs for your own good. Sing and make music to the Lord with your hearts. Always thank God the Father for everything in the name of our Lord Jesus Christ. (Ephesians 5:13–20, GW)

WHEN WE LIVE in a real relationship with God, we won't try to hide anything in our lives. Our relationships with others will be the same. Everything we do will be out in the open. That doesn't mean we do everything perfectly, though, and we'll still have to deal with our pride. But openness is evidence that the words of God are alive and active in us.

Some of the things I've done are very embarrassing. God shines His light not to expose them but to reveal the character that motivates me. While actions are easy to see, motivations can remain hidden.

This passage's call to wake up rings loudly in my heart. When His light reveals my motivations, I can begin to enjoy the beauty of Christ, the Messiah who redeems everything and makes it new. New motivations are born, new actions taken, and a thankful, peaceful presence rules in my heart.

> God's word is living and active. It is sharper than any two-edged sword and cuts as deep as the place where soul and spirit meet, the place where joints and marrow meet. God's word judges a person's thoughts and intentions. No creature can hide from God. Everything is uncovered and exposed for him to see. We must answer to him.
> We need to hold on to our declaration of faith: We have a superior chief priest who has gone through the heavens. That person is Jesus, the Son of God. (Hebrews 4:12–14, GW)

When I know the beauty of His light, and the power of all He says, I will be greatly motivated to stay where He is.

Day Ninety-Six
ONE THING THAT MATTERS

This is what the Lord of Heaven's Armies says: Look at what's happening to you! You have planted much but harvest little. You eat but are not satisfied. You drink but are still thirsty. You put on clothes but cannot keep warm. Your wages disappear as though you were putting them in pockets filled with holes!

This is what the Lord of Heaven's Armies says: Look at what's happening to you! Now go up into the hills, bring down timber, and rebuild my house. Then I will take pleasure in it and be honored, says the Lord. You hoped for rich harvests, but they were poor. And when you brought your harvest home, I blew it away. Why? Because my house lies in ruins, says the Lord of Heaven's Armies, while all of you are busy building your own fine houses. It's because of you that the heavens withhold the dew and the earth produces no crops. (Haggai 1:5–10, NLT)

HAGGAI WAS A prophet in Israel when many of the people returned to Jerusalem after having been held captive in Babylon. They had been called to return to Jerusalem and rebuild the temple.

But in the process, they got discouraged and oppressed. All the work stopped and nothing happened for many years. The people's lives became very difficult and they wouldn't change—that is, until God spoke these words to Haggai.

Then the people, and their leaders, responded to God's words and everything changed.

> So the Lord sparked the enthusiasm of Zerubbabel son of Shealtiel, governor of Judah, and the enthusiasm of Jeshua son of Jehozadak, the high priest, and the enthusiasm of the whole remnant of God's people. They began to work on the house of their God, the Lord of Heaven's Armies… (Haggai 1:14, NLT)

God has given us each a place and a purpose, but my response is sometimes the same as Israel's, focusing more on physical benefits than the purpose of God. When we choose that path, discouragement and oppression begin to suffocate us.

But there is a better way. Israel found it, and so can I.

The change started when God called for the people to wake up. He said, "Look at what's happening to you!" Something very important needed to happen. This was a wake-up call for the people to consider how they were living and use their energy to do the important work.

The emptiness I experience is directly related to my pursuit of empty ambitions. But when I direct my activities to honour God, I will experience full satisfaction. Doing His work is the one thing that always matters.

Day Ninety-Seven

EVIDENCE OF THE BRANCH

This is what the Lord of Heaven's Armies says: If you follow my ways and carefully serve me, then you will be given authority over my Temple and its courtyards. I will let you walk among these others standing here.

Listen to me, O Jeshua the high priest, and all you other priests. You are symbols of things to come. Soon I am going to bring my servant, the Branch. Now look at the jewel I have set before Jeshua, a single stone with seven facets. I will engrave an inscription on it, says the Lord of Heaven's Armies, and I will remove the sins of this land in a single day.

And on that day, says the Lord of Heaven's Armies, each of you will invite your neighbor to sit with you peacefully under your own grapevine and fig tree. (Zechariah 3:7–10, NLT)

GOD GIVES US so many blessings because of His love. Unfortunately, when we assume that God is motivated by our specialness, entitlement takes over and we brush aside our obligation to follow and carefully serve Him.

God spoke to His people through Zachariah, instructing them to follow His ways and serve with care in order to have influence and authority, eschewing ego-driven assumptions that could make it harder to hear and obey.

The people of Zachariah's day had important work to carry out, but that represents only a small picture of what God was doing. They were not the full expression of perfect servanthood. Someone was coming whose life of perfect service would free the people from everything that kept them from becoming true followers.

Jesus, the Branch, would do something never done before, something that would never need to be done again. This great event would be the removal of all the sin of the land in a single day.

> He himself is the sacrifice that atones for our sins—and not only our sins but the sins of all the world.
>
> And we can be sure that we know him if we obey his commandments. If someone claims, "I know God," but doesn't obey God's commandments, that person is a liar and is not living in the truth. But those who obey God's word truly show how completely they love him. That is how we know we are living in him. (1 John 2:2–5, NLT)

Being completely at peace with God, and my neighbour, is evidence that the work of the Branch has affected my life.

Day Ninety-Eight
THE INFLUENCE OF GOD'S ACTIONS

All praise to God, the Father of our Lord Jesus Christ, who has blessed us with every spiritual blessing in the heavenly realms because we are united with Christ. Even before he made the world, God loved us and chose us in Christ to be holy and without fault in his eyes. God decided in advance to adopt us into his own family by bringing us to himself through Jesus Christ. This is what he wanted to do, and it gave him great pleasure. So we praise God for the glorious grace he has poured out on us who belong to his dear Son. He is so rich in kindness and grace that he purchased our freedom with the blood of his Son and forgave our sins. He has showered his kindness on us, along with all wisdom and understanding. (Ephesians 1:3–8, NLT)

MANY UNSEEN EVENTS in our lives have a significant impact on the kind of people we become. These events may have nothing to do with our choices or preferences; they are planned and executed by God for a specific purpose. Some may be enjoyable, but others may be difficult, even painful. Just because something is a spiritual blessing doesn't mean it's necessarily pleasant, even though it comes from heavenly places.

When we understand God's attitude towards us during these times, we hold on to His grace and are changed, becoming all that He wants us to be. It's difficult to do the things He wants me to do without being the person He wants me to be.

David didn't do everything perfectly, but he saw the value of allowing God to plan every event in his life, both pleasant and painful, so he would become a person who fits perfectly into God's family: *"Before I suffered, I did wrong, but now I obey your word. You are good, and you do what is good. Teach me your demands"* (Psalm 119:67–68, NCV).

This is the work of His glorious grace, which He has so abundantly poured out on all those who belong to Jesus. This grace accompanies every difficult experience, making it possible for our lives to be changed.

The power of His grace changes my view of every difficulty I face. His grace doesn't take away the pain, but it does give me enough understanding to gain the full benefit. What is that benefit? His divine influence on my heart, which in turn is reflected in my life.

I live in freedom now, because of God's grace and the blood of Jesus.

Day Ninety-Nine
COME CLOSE WITH AN OPEN HEART AND MIND

And the Holy Spirit also bears witness to us; for after saying, "This is the covenant that I will make with them after those days, declares the Lord: I will put my laws on their hearts, and write them on their minds," then he adds, "I will remember their sins and their lawless deeds no more." Where there is forgiveness of these, there is no longer any offering for sin.

Therefore, brothers, since we have confidence to enter the holy places by the blood of Jesus, by the new and living way that he opened for us through the curtain, that is, through his flesh, and since we have a great priest over the house of God, let us draw near with a true heart in full assurance of faith, with our hearts sprinkled clean from an evil conscience and our bodies washed with pure water. Let us hold fast the confession of our hope without wavering, for he who promised is faithful. (Hebrews 10:15–23, ESV)

NONE OF US can duplicate God's way of doing His work. We can gain knowledge of His historical actions, but we know very little of all that God is. We know even less of what motivates Him to take action.

Unfortunately, our experience of lack can drive us to respond to Him in extreme ways. One way is to reject the fact that there is a God who cares about every detail of our lives. The opposite response is to make rules of conduct for every possible situation, assuming that He wants these rules to govern us.

Neither way brings life, but there is a very simple way to relate to God: *"Oh, the depth of the riches both of the wisdom and knowledge of God! How unsearchable are His judgments and His ways past finding out!"* (Romans 11:33, NKJV)

Every successful action is initiated by God. While I may not understand all His ways, I can know that He will complete everything He starts, going all the way back to His decision to make a covenant with mankind. This is true in the world He created, as well as in my personal life.

He makes my life free from sin, erasing all condemnation and opening the doors to freedom. In God's holy places, life is clean, and He opened them to me through the cleansing blood of Jesus.

God made all this possible, but He doesn't drag me here or demand perfection. The door is open and I can enter if I choose.

The most rewarding life is found when I simply come close to Him with my heart and mind open to everything He wants to do in me. I can be confident that it will happen, because He who made the promises always keeps them.

Day One Hundred

HIS WORDS ARE TRUE AND FAITHFUL

And I heard a great voice out of heaven saying, Behold, the tabernacle of God is with men, and he will dwell with them, and they shall be his people, and God himself shall be with them, and be their God. And God shall wipe away all tears from their eyes; and there shall be no more death, neither sorrow, nor crying, neither shall there be any more pain: for the former things are passed away. And he that sat upon the throne said, Behold, I make all things new. And he said unto me, Write: for these words are true and faithful. And he said unto me, It is done. I am Alpha and Omega, the beginning and the end. I will give unto him that is athirst of the fountain of the water of life freely. (Revelation 21:3–6, KJV)

OUR LIVES ARE mostly unpredictable, despite all our planning and preparation. We work hard, hoping to be free of trouble. We believe for good things to happen, but our lives often feature death, sorrow, and pain. And so we wonder, where is God? Does He even care about us? Does He exist at all?

These are legitimate questions and God will respond to them. His plan is to live among us, He as God and we as His people. That's when all the adversity is removed, for all the old things will be gone and everything made new. No enemy will survive the glory of Him living among us. There will be no dark place in which to hide. Death itself will be destroyed.

For he must reign, till he hath put all enemies under his feet. The last enemy that shall be destroyed is death. (1 Corinthians 15:25–26, KJV)

When words are spoken, we can forget them and never think of them again, but the same isn't true for words that are written down. God wanted His words written down because they are true and will be faithfully completed. He doesn't want us to forget them.

When He says, *"It is done,"* we should have no question about its completion, even though our eyes don't see it yet. All the actions He has promised have already been completed in the realms of heaven—and one day they will be active and visible on the earth.

He invites us to participate in this new life. He invites us to have Him as our God. When we do, we'll discover eternal life and an end to pain. We will have a new beginning and death will be destroyed. It will happen because He said so.

ALSO BY JOHN TROYER

ISBN: 978-1-4866-2494-2

One of the greatest motivators in life is joy. When joy is at the root of your actions, your work will give you great satisfaction. Whether you work as a tradesperson in a shop, or sit in an office, or serve in a church, the joy inside you will set you apart from the rest of the world.

This devotional contains lessons derived from the stories and people written about in the Bible, as well as the real-life experiences of the author. What is your story?

ISBN: 978-1-4866-2598-7

Most of us came to Jesus because of a desperate need, just like those in Bible times, and He gave us what we asked for. Our lives were changed! Unfortunately, our focus on the self easily drives us to selfishly use what He gives us.

Jesus changed the lives of everyone who came to Him, but not everyone responded the same way. Some fell on their

knees and worshipped Him while others didn't even stop to thank Him. But there were a few who were so awed by this Man that they gave up everything to follow, denying themselves to serve Him.

What's your response to what Jesus did for you?

ISBN: 978-1-4866-2507-9

This is my story of growing up in a small town in Nebraska, often looking at maps of northern Canada and dreaming of going there. Those dreams eventually came true, but first I had to undertake a journey from angry unbelief and rebellion to complete confidence and surrender to God, who gave me a purpose.

The resulting saga took me from Tuktoyaktuk in the Northwest Territories, on the shore of the Arctic Ocean, to the jungles of South America. But the most exciting adventure has been my faith walk and really knowing what it's like to have the hand of God on my shoulder protecting, directing, and correcting me.

The journey continues.

www.ingramcontent.com/pod-product-compliance
Lightning Source LLC
Chambersburg PA
CBHW060517100426
42743CB00009B/1350